PETER MERIAN HAUS BASEL

Hans Zwimpfer

PETER MERIAN HAUS BASEL

An der Schnittstelle von Kunst, Technik und Architektur
At the Interface between Art, Technology and Architecture

Fotografien/Photographs: Margherita Spiluttini

Birkhäuser – Publishers for Architecture
Basel · Boston · Berlin

Textredaktion/Editing: Franziska Baetcke
Übersetzung ins Englische/Translation into English:
Katja Steiner and Bruce Almberg, Ehingen
Layout/Design: Christoph Kloetzli, Basel

Fotografien/Photographs: Margherita Spiluttini, Wien/Vienna
mit Ausnahme von S. 44, 45/with exception of pp. 44, 45: Sidney Bannier, Basel

A CIP catalogue record for this book is available from the Library
of Congress, Washington D.C., USA.

Die Deutsche Bibliothek - CIP-Einheitsaufnahme

Peter-Merian-Haus Basel : an der Schnittstelle von Kunst,
Technik und Architektur / Hans Zwimpfer. [Textred.: Franziska
Baetcke. Übers. ins Engl.: Katja Steiner and Bruce Almberg]. -
Basel ; Boston ; Berlin : Birkhäuser, 2002
   ISBN 3-7643-6621-4

This work is subject to copyright. All rights are reserved, whether
the whole or part of the material is concerned, specifically the
rights of translation, reprinting, re-use of illustrations, recitation,
broadcasting, reproduction on microfilms or in other ways, and
storage in data bases.
For any kind of use permission of the copyright owner must be
obtained.

© 2002 Birkhäuser – Publishers for Architecture, P.O. Box 133,
  CH-4010 Basel, Switzerland.
  Member of the BertelsmannSpringer Publishing Group.

Printed on acid-free paper produced of chlorine-free pulp. TCF ∞
Printed in Germany

ISBN 3-7643-6621-4

9 8 7 6 5 4 3 2 1

http://www.birkhauser.ch

INHALT

7 Ein Haus setzt ein Zeichen
23 Kunst und Architektur am Peter Merian Haus
67 1+1=3 oder Erfahrungen mit «Kunst und Architektur»
75 Planungs- und Baugeschichte

  Anhang
83 Bautechnik, Statik, Fassade
87 Technische Daten / Kosten
92 Beteiligte Künstlerinnen und Künstler
93 1986–2000 Planung / Bauherrschaft / Eigentümer / Mieter

CONTENTS

7 A Building Lights the Way
23 Art and Architecture at Peter Merian Haus
67 1+1=3 or: Experience of "Art and Architecture"
75 Planning and Building History

  Appendix
83 Constructional Engineering, Statics, Façade
87 Technical Data / Cost
92 Participating Artists
93 1986–2000 Planning / Clients / Owners / Tenants

EIN HAUS SETZT EIN ZEICHEN

Das Peter Merian Haus steht mitten in Basel, und obwohl Basel keine grosse Stadt ist, mutet dieser Standort grossstädtisch an. Da ist rechts das breite Gleisfeld in der Einfahrt zum Bahnhof, links die Kreuzung von zwei stark befahrenen, innerstädtischen Verkehrsachsen, gegenüber einige neuere Verwaltungsgebäude und eine abgasgeschwärzte Restzeile der alten Blockrandbebauung. Der Ort ist vom Verkehr bestimmt. Wie ein Eisberg ragt aus diesem Meer von Zügen, Autos, Strassenbahnen und Fussgängern das Peter Merian Haus auf – grün schimmernd, kühl, sein Äusseres mit jeder Witterung wechselnd.

Das Haus ist nicht zu übersehen, was zweifellos an seiner Grösse liegt: Es ist 180 Meter lang und 60 Meter breit. Schon auf den ersten Blick wird klar, dass dieses Haus ohne Schnickschnack auskommt. Jedes Kind kann es beschreiben. Es ist aus einer sich sechsfach wiederholenden Abfolge von Haus und Hof zusammengesetzt. Fast scheint es, als sei der rechtwinklige Raster des karierten Papiers, auf dem es entworfen wurde, noch in der dreidimensionalen Umsetzung wieder zu erkennen. Die minimale architektonische Gestaltung lässt Freiraum für Inhalte, für Kunst. Das Peter Merian Haus ist mehr als die Summe seiner vier Fassadenseiten, obwohl es natürlich auch eine Fassade hat: Sie ist aus rechteckigen Glasplatten zusammengesetzt und umfasst den Baukörper wie eine Haut. Die visuelle Logik der Fassade wird aber nicht wie ein Taschenspielertrick an der Oberfläche des Gebauten erkennbar, sondern ist bereits im Inneren angelegt, in der Anordnung der Räume. Das ist das Gesetz dieser Architektur: den Bedürfnissen ihrer Benutzer zu dienen, den Menschen, die hier arbeiten und lernen und ihre Tage hier verbringen. Das vor allem zeichnet das Peter Merian Haus aus.

Das Gebäude trägt keine Handschrift, kein Design. Imagebildung ist hier Sache der Kunst. Acht internationale Künstlerinnen und Künstler sind mit grossen Werken am Peter Merian Haus beteiligt. Weitere künstlerische Interventionen haben das Bauprojekt in seinem Entstehen begleitet. Dies alles erfolgte in direkter und enger Zusammenarbeit zwi-

A BUILDING LIGHTS THE WAY

Peter Merian House is located in the center of Basel, at a site that suggests Basel is a larger city than it actually is. To the right, a wide expanse of railway tracks enters the station, to the left two busy inner-city traffic routes intersect, and on the opposite side of the road are a few fairly modern administrative buildings and the remaining buildings of the old perimeter development, blackened by exhaust fumes. The location is defined by the traffic. Like an iceberg, Peter Merian House rises above a sea of trains, cars, trams and pedestrians – shimmering green, cool, its exterior changing with each shift in the weather.

At 180 meters long and 60 meters wide, the structure is too big to be ignored. The observer immediately realizes that this building scorns superfluous details. A child could describe it. It is composed of a sequence of six buildings and atria. The grid of the graph paper on which it was drafted almost seems to be present in the three-dimensional realization. The minimalist architectural design leaves space for content, for art. Peter Merian House is more than the sum of its four façades, although of course it does have a façade, composed of rectangular glass panels and embracing the building volume like a shell. The visual logic of the façade, however, is not revealed on the surface of the construction by some sleight of hand, but is anchored inside, in the arrangement of the spaces. This is the law governing this architecture: to serve the requirements of its users, the people who work and study here, who occupy their time here in various ways. This, above all, is what characterizes Peter Merian House.

The building bears no signature, no design. Establishing an image is an artistic matter here. Eight international artists have provided large-scale works for Peter Merian House. Other artistic interventions accompanied the building project throughout its development. All of this involved direct and close collaboration between the artists and the architects, to engage with an issue that is endemic in contemporary architecture and realize it consistently: the search for a new symbiosis

schen den Künstlerinnen und Künstlern und den Architekten. Damit ist ein Thema aufgegriffen worden, das in der zeitgenössischen Architektur virulent ist und das hier konsequent ausgeführt wurde. Hier ist nach einer neuen Symbiose von Kunst und Architektur gesucht worden, nach gegenseitiger Herausforderung und Beflügelung, nach wechselweiser Klärung und Durchdringung. Die Übersetzung der inneren Organisation in eine abwechselnd matte und transparente Glashaut etwa wurde zusammen mit dem amerikanischen Künstler Donald Judd erarbeitet. Die Fassade ist überhaupt das Paradestück der erträumten Integration von Kunst und Architektur. An ihr ist der Anteil der Kunst nicht ablösbar. Die Fassade ist Kunst, und dennoch ist das Gebäude nicht einfach ein begehbares Riesenkunstwerk. Vielmehr bietet es der Kunst Raum, bleibt dabei aber ein Haus, nüchtern und funktionsorientiert, wie es sich für ein Geschäftsgebäude gehört.

Das Peter Merian Haus setzt an einem schwierigen Ort ein städtebauliches Signal. Es verspricht Nutzung und Arbeitsplätze, wo vorher nichts war. Mehr noch: Die Architekten und Ingenieure, die an diesem Neubau beteiligt waren, setzten im Bereich von Statik, Innenausbau und Ökologie auf neue Lösungen. Das Haus ist als Edelrohbau konzipiert. Die Räume sind durchgehend drei Meter hoch, der Innenausbau ist minimal. Das bedeutet ganz konkret: keine Verkleidungen der Stützen, keine herabgehängten Decken, keine pauschalen Beleuchtungssysteme. Wo sich die Fenster auf einen Hof hin öffnen lassen, wurde auch auf die Klimaanlage verzichtet. Auf dem Dach wachsen Pflanzen aus einer Humusschicht. Sie fangen Flugrost auf und produzieren Sauerstoff. Die Erde wiederum staut Regenwasser, das für die Toilettenspülung wieder verwendet wird.

Auch bauökonomisch wurden die Zeichen der Zeit erkannt. Aus ähnlich grossen Projekten hatte man gelernt, dass nur ein Bauen in Etappen, in diesem Fall also blockweise, Erfolg versprechend ist. So konnte die Finanzierung schrittweise gesichert werden, und das Unterfangen ge-

between art and architecture, a mutual challenge and inspiration, an alternate clarification and permeation. The translation of the inner organization into an alternately matte and transparent glass shell, for example, was elaborated together with the American artist Donald Judd. The façade is a showpiece for the integrated vision of art and architecture. The role that art plays in it is irreplaceable. The façade is art, and yet the building is not simply a giant work of art you can walk into. Rather, it provides space for art, but remains a building – sober and functional, as befits a commercial construction.

Peter Merian House blazes an urban trail in a problematic place. It offers usefulness and jobs in a location where previously there was nothing. Furthermore, the architects and engineers who participated in this new building relied on new solutions in the fields of statics, interior design and ecology. The building was conceived as a noble shell. All the spaces are three meters high; the interior fixtures are kept to a minimum. This means that there is no disguise for the supports, no suspended ceilings, no industrial lighting systems. Where windows can be opened on an atrium, there is no air conditioning. On the roof, plants grow in a layer of humus. They catch films of rust and produce oxygen. The soil collects rainwater, which is reused for flushing the toilets.

Signs of the times were also recognized in the building economics. Similar large-scale projects had taught that building in stages, in this case in blocks, was the way to succeed. The financing for the project could also be secured in stages, and despite the volatile economy was never seriously at risk. At times, Hans Zwimpfer, who initiated and promoted Peter Merian House, would have preferred to call a halt, but not because of problems of technological or financial feasibility. Rather, it was the additional burden that Hans Zwimpfer has shouldered for himself and Peter Merian House: to prove that artists and architects still have something to say, that artists are willing and able to comply with the demands of architecture, and that architects are willing and able to

riet trotz schwankender Konjunktur nie ernsthaft in Gefahr. Wenn Hans Zwimpfer, der das Peter Merian Haus initiiert und vorangetrieben hat, bis es vollendet war, hin und wieder – selten, aber es kam doch vor – den ganzen Krempel am liebsten hingeschmissen hätte, dann nicht wegen technischer oder finanzieller Schwierigkeiten. Vielmehr hatte er sich und dem Peter Merian Haus eine zusätzliche Last auferlegt: Es galt zu beweisen, dass sich Künstler und Architekten noch etwas zu sagen haben, dass sich Künstler in die Zwänge des Bauens einspannen lassen und Architekten freie Kunst in ihre Pläne aufnehmen können und wollen. Ohne diese zusätzliche Aufgabe wäre vieles leichter gewesen: Zeit, Nerven und auch etwas Geld hätten gespart werden können. Andererseits gäbe es dann auch keinen Anlass, dieses Buch zu publizieren.

Darüber hinaus ist zu beachten, dass das Peter Merian Haus gerade im Hinblick auf die Integration von Kunst als Vorspiel und Vorbild für ein Projekt verstanden wird, das ab 1.1.2002 direkt nebenan entsteht. Das Jacob Burckhardt Haus soll die Erfahrungen fortsetzen und zu einem weiteren Exempel für einen innovativen Umgang mit Material, Technik, Umwelt und die wegweisende Integration von Kunst und Architektur werden.

integrate free art into their plans. Without this additional requirement many things would have been easier: time, nerves and some money would have been saved. But this interaction between art and architecture is the reason behind the publication of this book.

Moreover, in its integration of art Peter Merian House is a precursor and model for a project to be constructed next to it, starting in January 2002. Jacob Burckhardt House will build on previous experience and provide another example of the innovative handling of material, technology and environment, and the trendsetting integration of art and architecture.

KUNST UND ARCHITEKTUR AM PETER MERIAN HAUS

FASSADE | Donald Judd (in Zusammenarbeit mit den Architekten)

Der amerikanische Künstler Donald Judd (1928–1994), einer der Hauptvertreter der Minmal Art, war für die Fassadengestaltung engagiert worden, als es auf den Plänen noch keine Fassade gab, und lange bevor der erste Spatenstich getan war. Donald Judds Plastiken faszinierten die Architekten. Gleichzeitig war Judd selbst stark an Architektur interessiert. Erstaunlicherweise war er aber noch nie an einem grösseren architektonischen Projekt beteiligt gewesen. Bei den gemeinsamen Sitzungen im Frühjahr 1993 in Basel stellt sich umgehend heraus, dass zwischen dem Künstler und den Architekten die Chemie stimmt. Judd lässt sich in die Planung einweihen, vertieft sich in die architektonischen Gegebenheiten und entwickelt Vorschläge hinsichtlich Material und Struktur der Fassade. Drei Dinge sind ihm besonders wichtig: Das Haus soll klare und eindeutige Linien tragen, es soll in sich geschlossen sein, und es soll seine innere Struktur nach aussen sichtbar machen. Diese Prämissen können am Peter Merian Haus direkt umgesetzt werden. Zentrales Element ist die Glashaut, die das Haus zusammenhält, ihm seine Kontur gibt und durch ihre Abfolge von matt gefärbten und durchsichtigen Glasscheiben die Struktur des Hauses mit dem Wechselspiel von Haus und Hof transparent macht. So markant die Fassade ist, so auffällig sie das Haus kleidet, so durchlässig ist sie auch, spiegelt sie doch keine Verhältnisse vor, die nicht auch im Inneren anzutreffen wären. Das macht aus dem Peter Merian Haus eine von der Minimal Art geprägte Plastik – die grösste und leider auch die letzte, die Donald Judd mitentworfen hat.

ART AND ARCHITECTURE AT PETER MERIAN HOUSE

FAÇADE | Donald Judd (in collaboration with the architects)

The American artist Donald Judd (1928–1994), one of the leading exponents of minimalist art, was commissioned at a point when the plans did not contain a façade and long before the cornerstone was laid. The architects were fascinated by Donald Judd's sculptures. Judd himself had a strong interest in architecture, but had never before participated in a large-scale architectonic project. During meetings in Basel in the spring of 1993, the chemistry between the artist and the architects was immediately apparent. Judd was initiated into the planning, immersed himself in the architectural conditions and developed proposals for the material and structure of the façade. Three things were of special importance to him: the structure should have clear lines, be self-contained, and should have an internal organization visible from the outside. All these ideas could be realized in Peter Merian House. The central element is the glass shell that holds the building together, provides its distinctive contour and makes its structure – the interaction between building and atrium – visible through its sequence of matte and transparent glass panels. Striking though the façade is, and as distinctly as it "clothes" the building, it is permeable, reflecting nothing to mask what can be found within. This is what makes Peter Merian House a kind of sculpture influenced by minimal art – the largest and unfortunately also the last that Donald Judd co-designed.

FUSSGÄNGERPASSAGE | Roni Horn, «Yous in You»
(Bodenplatten in Beton und Gummi, Sitzbänke)

In der 180 Meter langen, öffentlichen Fussgängerpassage bewegt sich der Passant auf unsicherem Grund. Der Weg ist mit Bodenplatten aus Beton und Gummi in zwei verschiedenen Härtegraden ausgelegt. Optisch sind dabei nur die Unterschiede zwischen Beton (grau) und Gummi (orange) ersichtlich. Das unterschiedlich sanfte Federn auf den Gummiplatten wird erst erfahren, wenn man sie betritt. Das ist ungewohnt und angenehm. Es ist, als befände man sich plötzlich an einem ganz anderen Ort – vielleicht in Island, woher ja auch das Muster der Bodenplatten stammt. Die Arbeit «Yous in You» verhält sich zur Fassade wie ein Kontrapunkt. Während das türkise Haus eher kühl wirkt, strahlen die orangen Bodenplatten Wärme aus. Geometrisch ist die Formensprache des Baus, organisch die des Kunstwerks, das man nicht primär mit den Augen wahrnehmen kann, sondern mit dem Körper, taktil, erfährt.

Roni Horn, geboren 1955, lebt und arbeitet in New York und Island.

PEDESTRIAN PASSAGE | Roni Horn, "Yous in You"
(floor panels in concrete and rubber, benches)

In the 180-meter-long public pedestrian passage the passers-by move on uncertain ground: the floor panels covering the walkway are made of concrete and rubber, in two different degrees of hardness. The only detectable visual difference between the concrete (gray) and the rubber (orange) panels is their color. The elasticity of the rubber panels can be experienced only by stepping on them. It is unusual, and rather comfortable. It is as though one were suddenly in a totally different place – Iceland, perhaps, where the pattern of the floor panels originates. The work "Yous in You" is like a counterpoint to the façade. The turquoise building has a rather cool effect, whereas the orange floor panels radiate warmth. The language of the building is geometric; the artwork – which is primarily perceived by the body rather than the eyes – is tactile, is organic.

Roni Horn, born in 1955, lives and works in New York and Iceland.

HAUS 80, LICHTHOF | Brigitte Kowanz, «Light is what we see»
(Glas, Schrift, Licht)

Alle Aufmerksamkeit richtet sich auf die Glaswand, die den Lichthof und die angrenzenden Büroräumlichkeiten voneinander trennt und doch miteinander verbindet. Über diese Glaswand verläuft, einmal ab- und einmal aufsteigend, der Satz «Light is what we see» (Licht ist, was wir sehen). Die Anzahl und die Anordnung der Buchstaben nimmt auf die vorhandenen Glasscheiben Bezug. Der Satz passt genau – auch im übertragenen Sinn, denn dass wir ihn sehen, verdanken wir dem Licht, das sich in ihm bricht und das wir gleichzeitig mit dem Satz und seiner Bedeutung wahrnehmen.

Brigitte Kowanz, geboren 1957, lebt und arbeitet in Wien.

BUILDING 80, ATRIUM | Brigitte Kowanz, "Light is what we see"
(glass, script, light)

All attention is directed at the glass wall that separates and connects the atrium and the adjoining offices. The sentence "Light is what we see" runs up and down this glass wall twice, once descending and once ascending. The number and arrangement of the letters refers to the number of glass panels. The meaning of the sentence is perfect too: we see it because of the light that it breaks up, and that we perceive simultaneously with the sentence and its meaning.

Brigitte Kowanz, born in 1957, lives and works in Vienna.

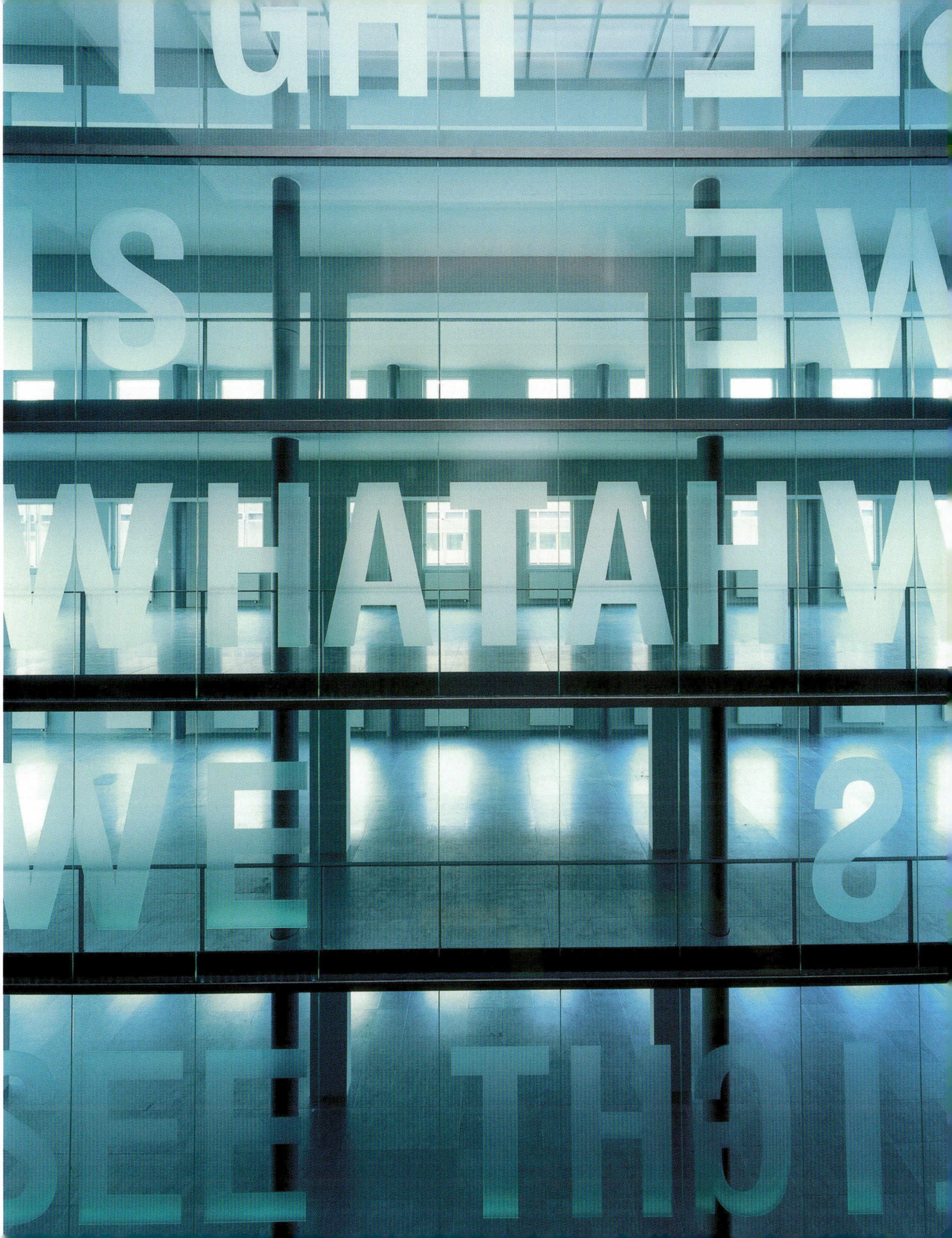

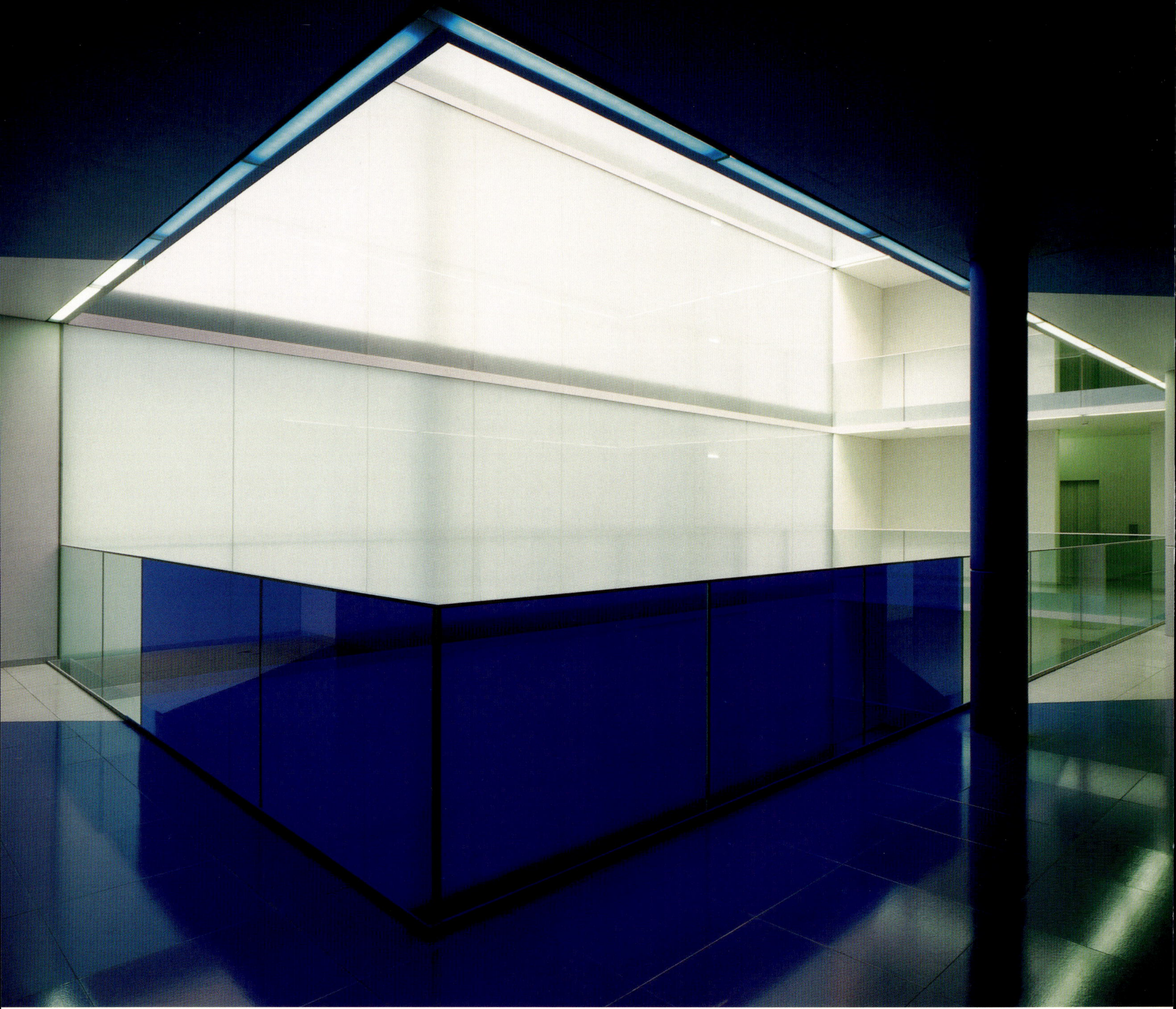

HAUS 82, LICHTHOF | Ursula Mumenthaler, «Le champ bleu»
(Acrylfarbe Lascaux 119, kobaltblau)

Die blaue Farbe verschluckt eine Raumecke. Ausgehend von der Grundfläche eines Dreiecks, zieht sich das Blau fünf Stockwerke hoch und färbt alles, was seinen Weg kreuzt: die Wände, die Decken, den Boden, die Brüstung, den Handlauf, das Licht und selbst die Lichtschalter, alles ist blau. Das Blau nimmt dem Raum die Tiefenschärfe und durchkreuzt die rechtwinklige Ordnung der Architektur. Das blaue Farbfeld zieht eine Diagonale quer durch den Raum, der dadurch seine geometrische Strenge verliert.

Ursula Mumenthaler, geboren 1955, lebt und arbeitet in Genf.

BUILDING 82, ATRIUM | Ursula Mumenthaler, "Le champ bleu"
(acrylic paint Lascaux 119, cobalt blue)

The blue color swallows a corner of the space. Starting with a basic triangular surface, the blue climbs up five floors and colors everything that crosses its path: the walls, the ceilings, the floor, the parapet, the railing, the light and even the light switches – everything is blue. The blue takes the depth of field from the space and crosses the rectangular order of the architecture. The blue color field draws a diagonal across the space, which loses its geometric rigidity as a result.

Ursula Mumenthaler, born in 1955, lives and works in Geneva.

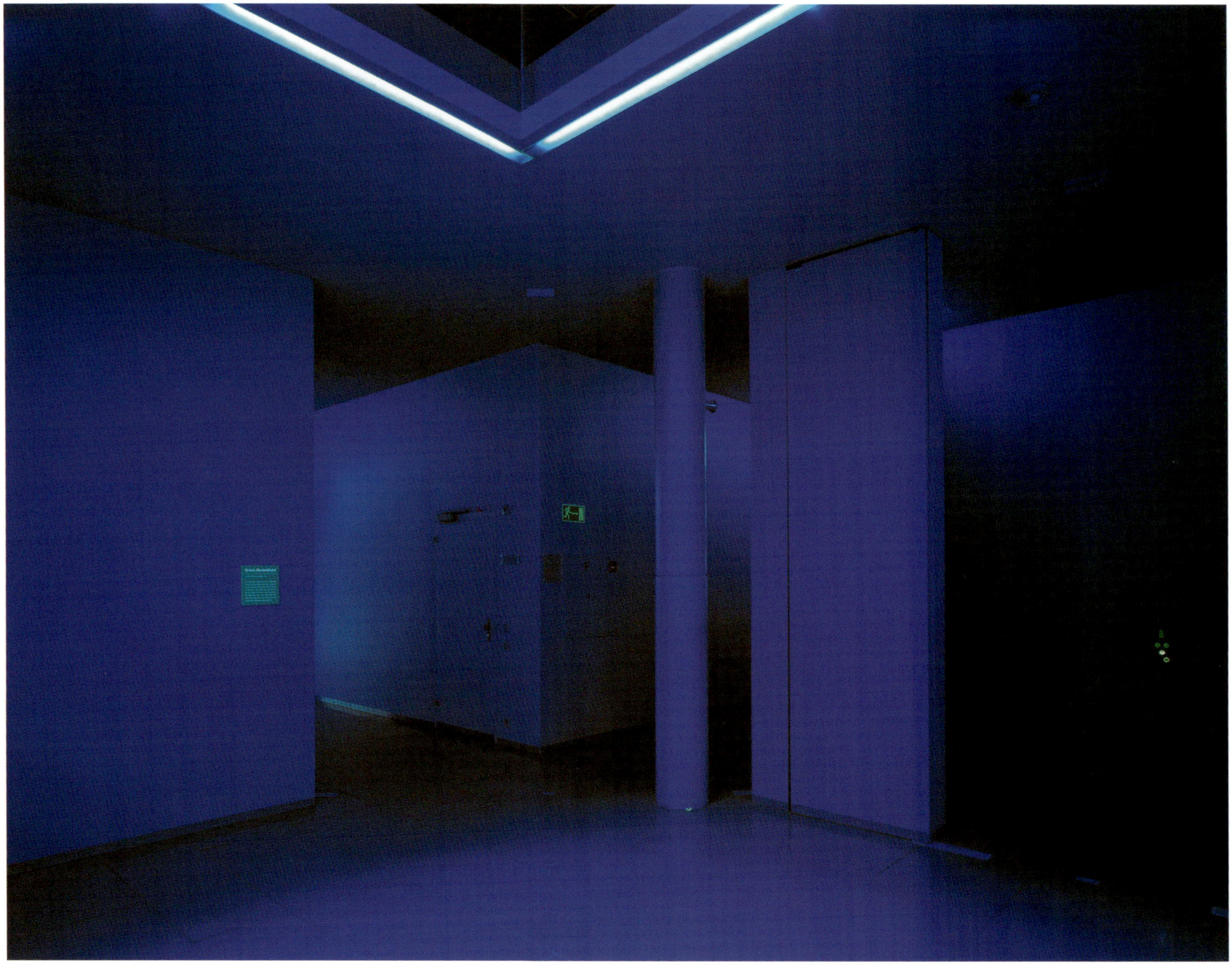

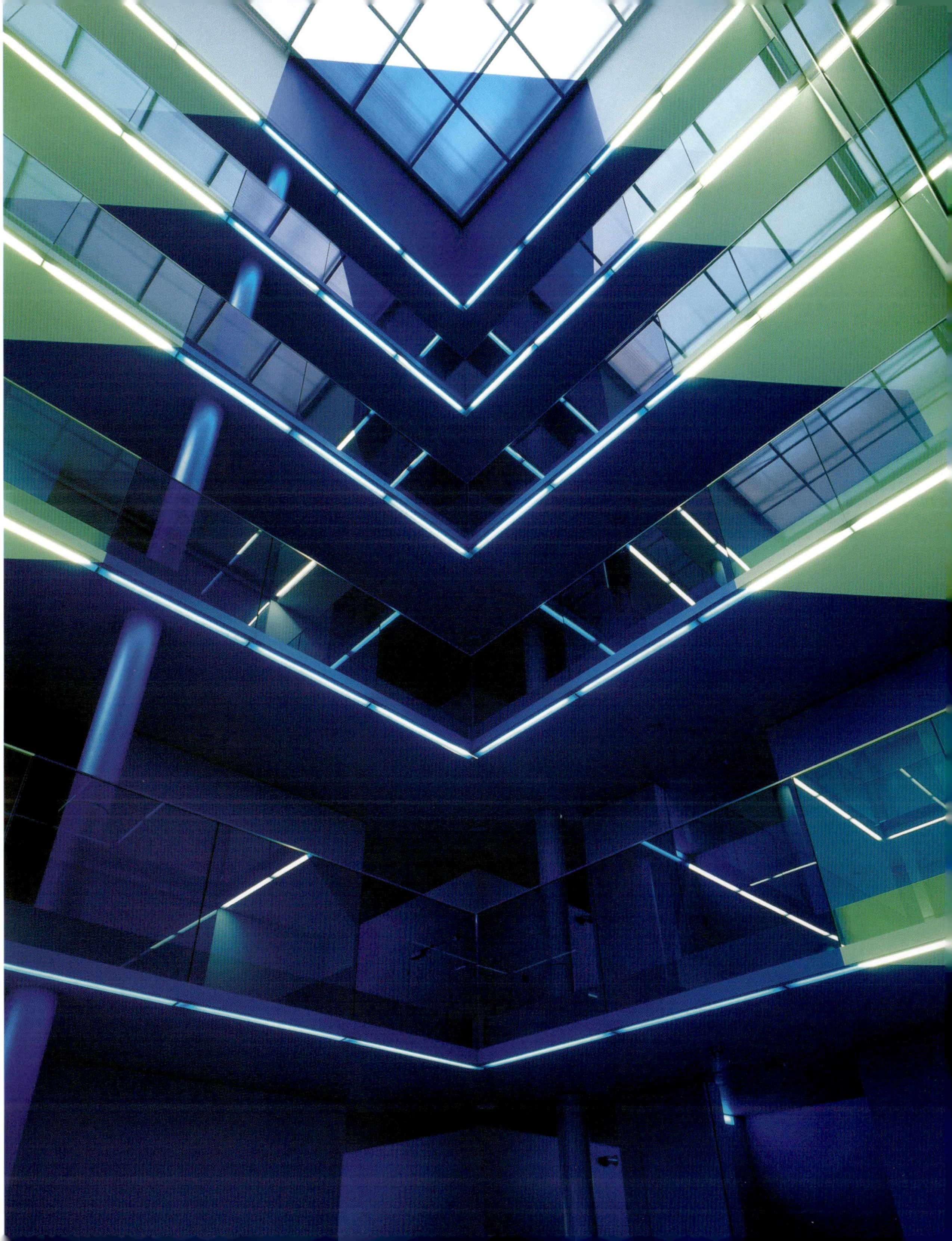

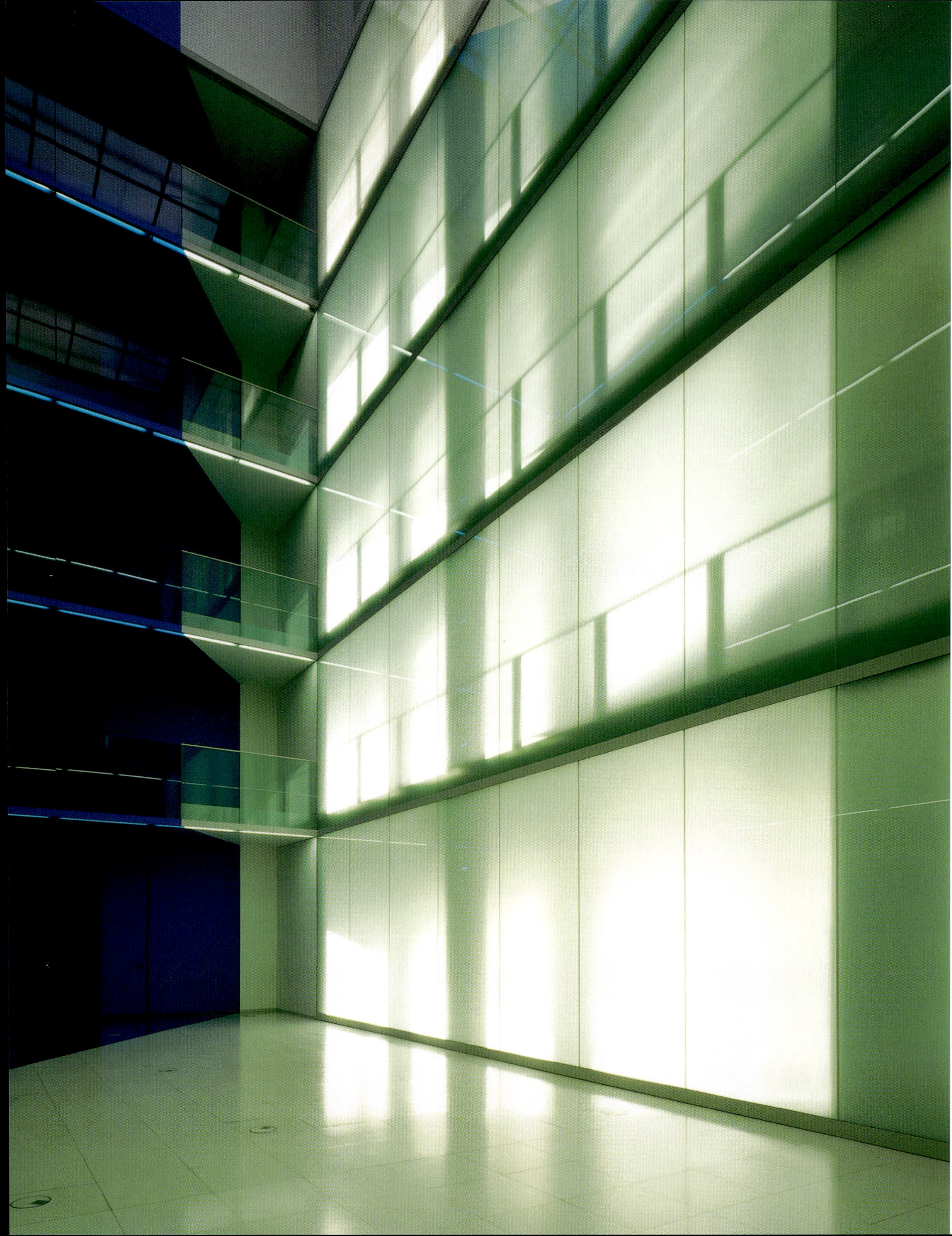

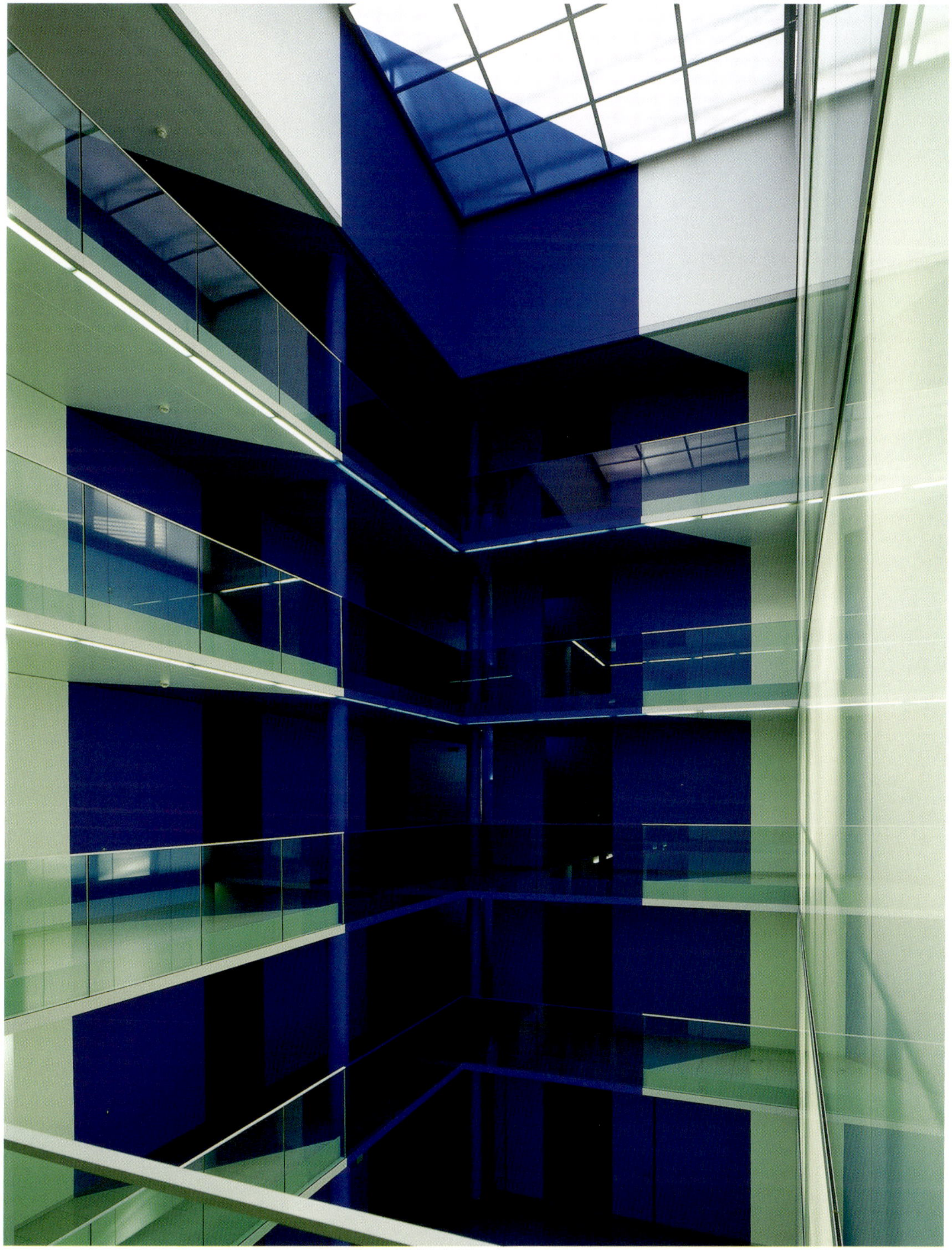

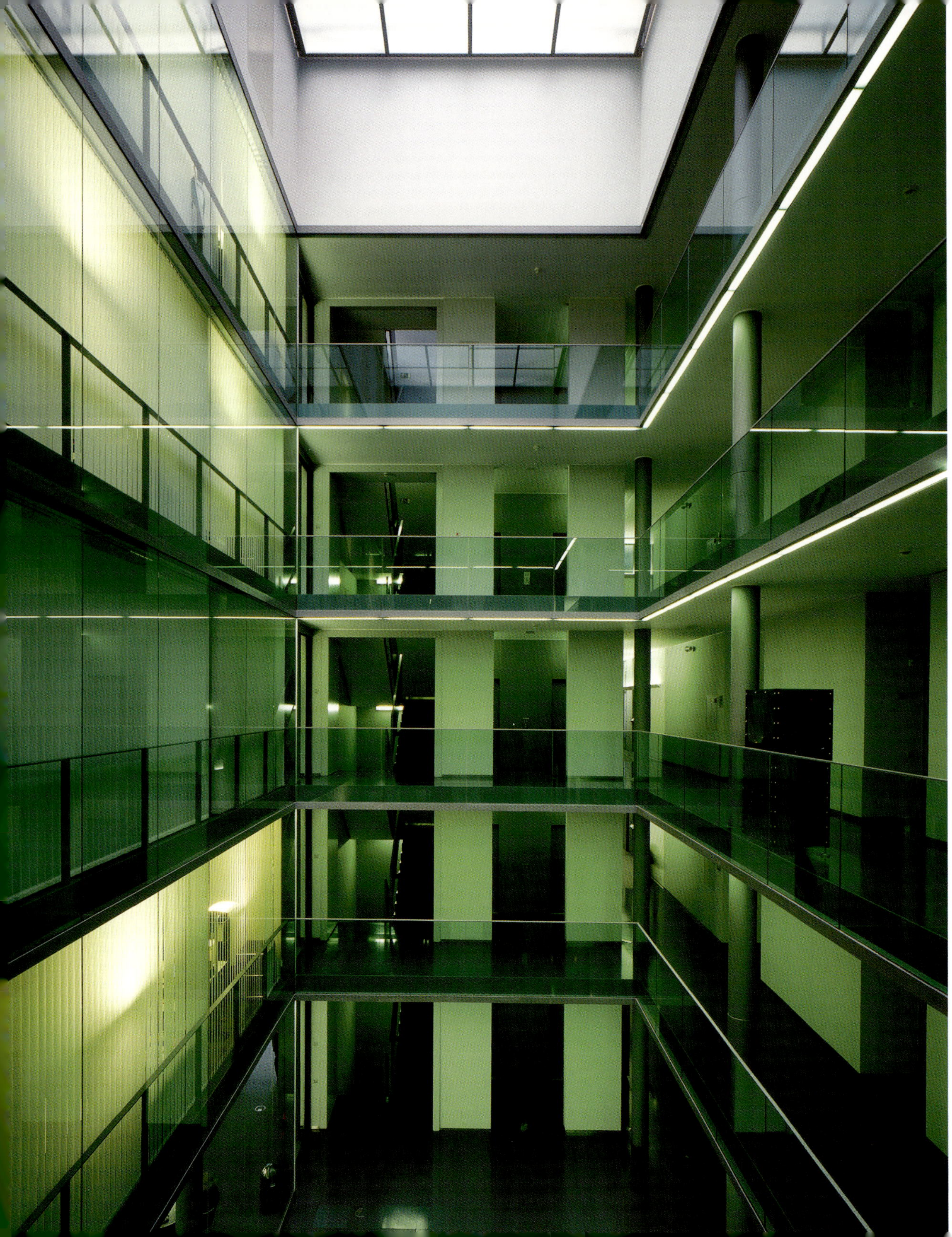

HAUS 84, LICHTHOF | Pipilotti Rist, «Geist des Stroms» (Mixed Media)

Dieses Haus ist verhext. Seine Geister wohnen auf Festplatten und in Glasfaserkabeln. Den grössten Teil des Tages sind sie unsichtbar. Aber sie haben einen festen Stundenplan: Fünfmal täglich, um 8.00, 13.00, 17.00, 21.00 und 24.00 Uhr (an den Wochenenden exklusiv zur Geisterstunde), treten sie für wenige Sekunden in Erscheinung. Der ganze Spuk besteht aus optischen und akustischen Erscheinungen, die im 2., 3., 4. und 5. Geschoss sowie im Lift ihren festen Platz haben. Die optischen Gespenstererscheinungen werden auf Monitoren, die so klein wie Steckdosen sind, oder auf einer ganz gewöhnlichen Wand sichtbar. Während eine von ihnen fortwährend Blasen speit, ertönen die akustischen Erscheinungen aus 12 über alle Etagen verteilten Lautsprechern.

Pipilotti Rist, geboren 1962, lebt und arbeitet in Zürich.

BUILDING 84, ATRIUM | Pipilotti Rist, "Geist des Stroms" (mixed media)

This building is bewitched: spirits live in hard drives and fiber optic cables. Invisible for most of the day, they have a firmly established schedule: they appear for a few seconds five times a day, at 8 a.m., 1, 5, 9 p.m. and midnight (on weekends, only at the witching hour). The visual and acoustic phantoms have fixed locations on the 3rd, 4th, 5th and 6th floors, as well as in the elevator. The ghostly apparitions become visible on monitors, which can be as small as an electrical socket, or as projections on ordinary walls. One of them continuously spews out bubbles; the acoustic apparitions utter sounds from 12 speakers distributed throughout the floors.

Pipilotti Rist, born in 1962, lives and works in Zurich.

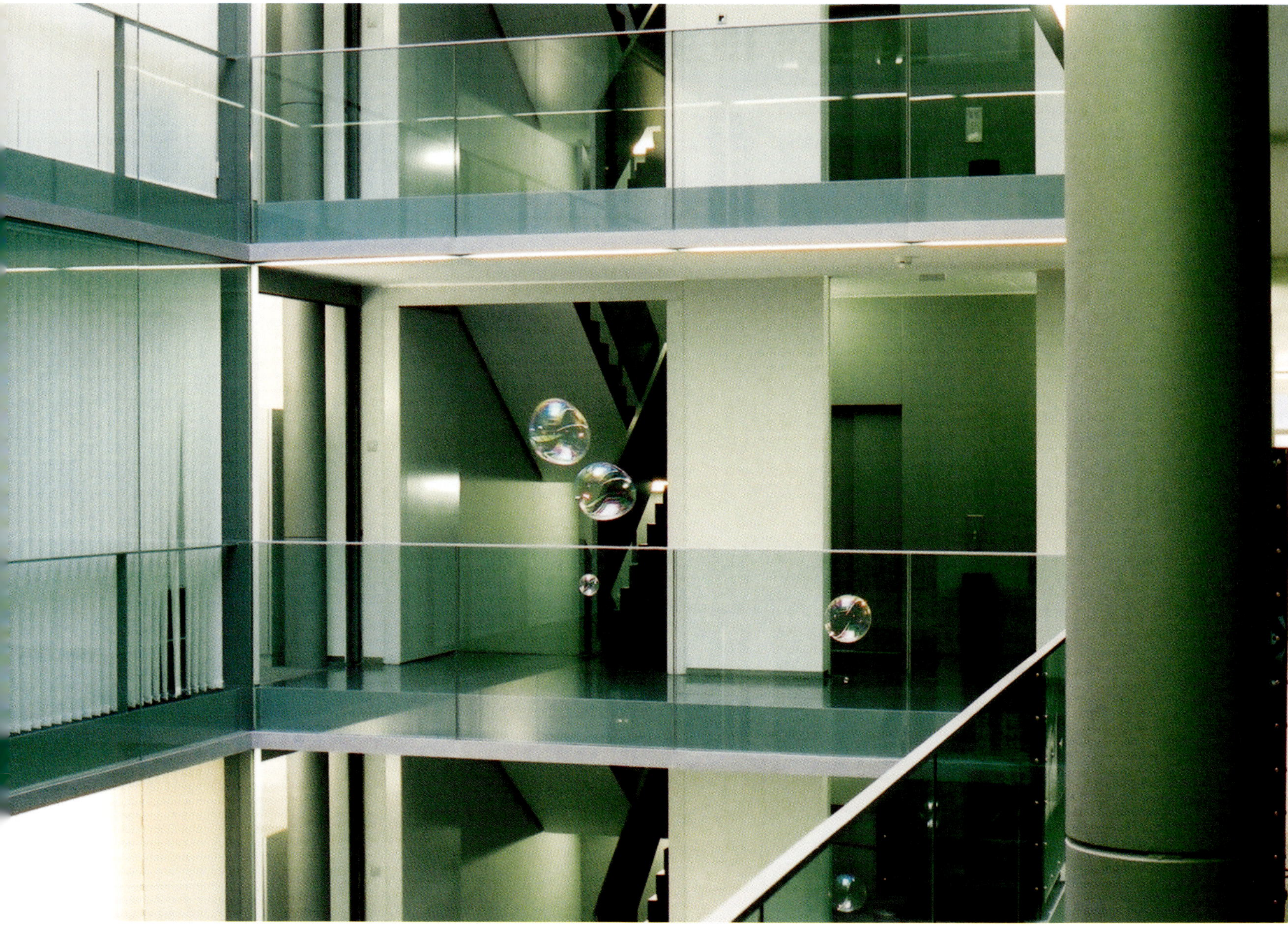

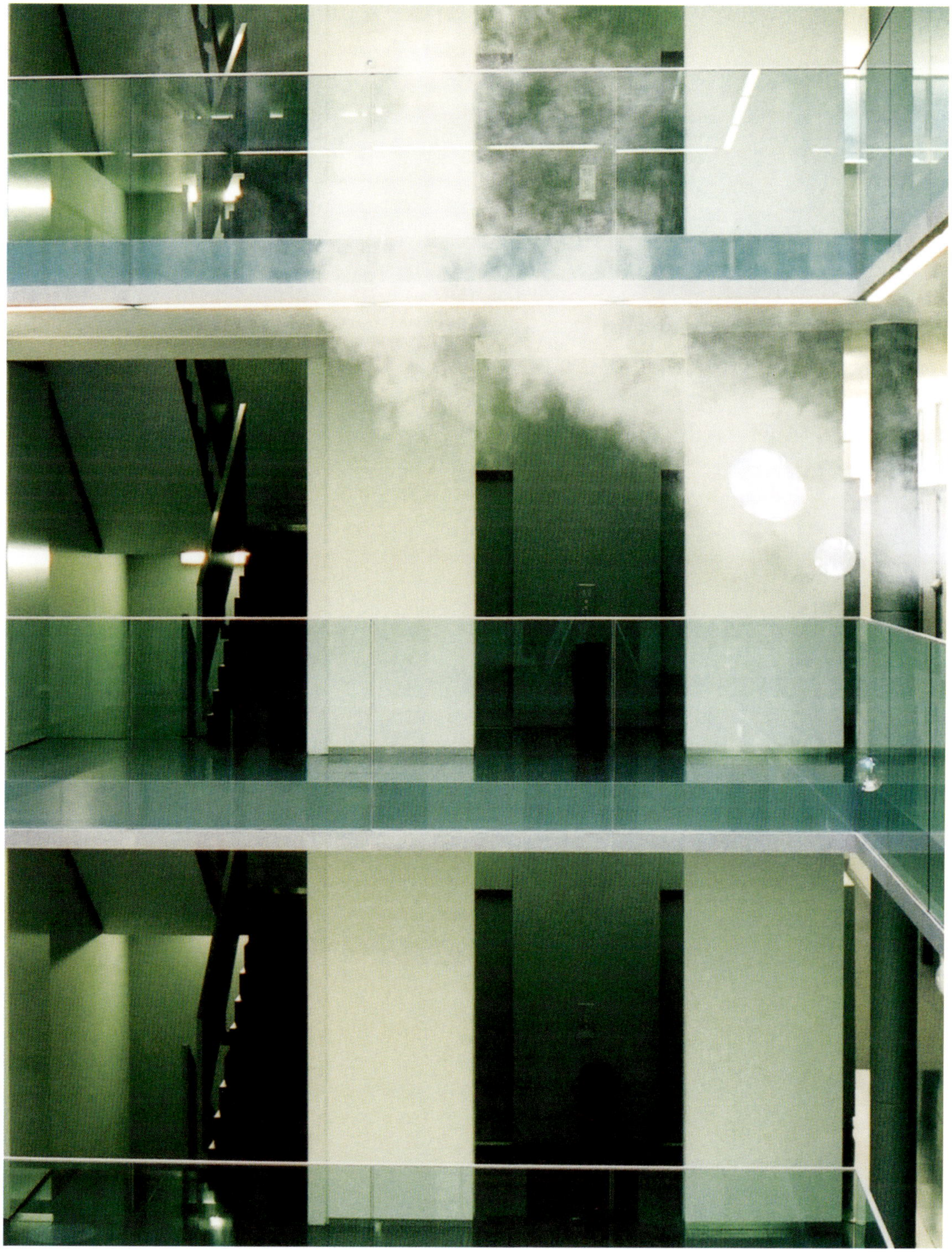

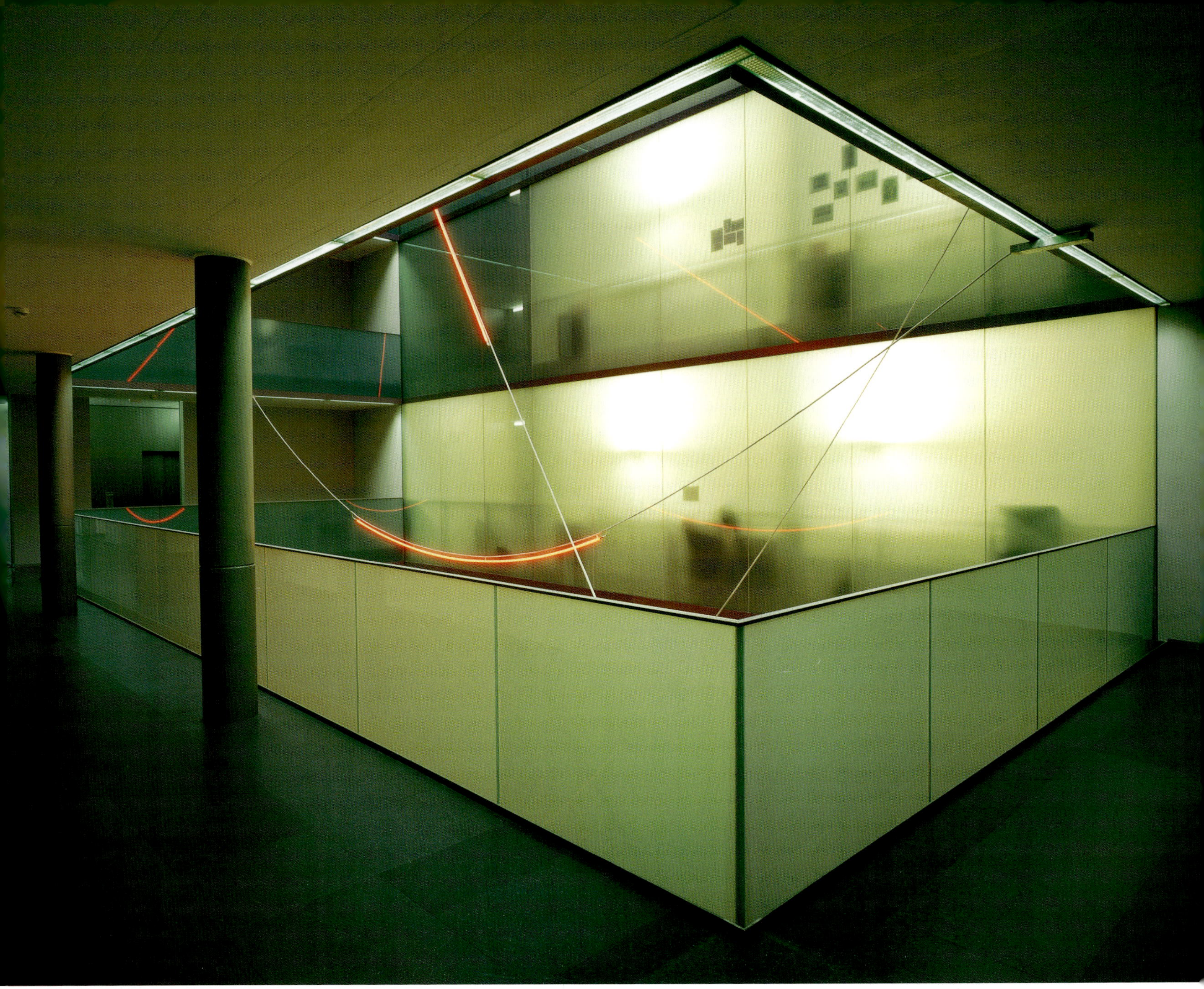

HAUS 86, LICHTHOF UND TREPPE | François Morellet, «Bogen, Sehne, Licht» (Neonröhren, Stahlseile) und «Bogen, Sehne, Strich» (Digitalprints, Plexiglas, Neonlicht)

Drei rote Neonschläuche hängen im Inneren des Lichthofs. Zwei von ihnen beschreiben einen Bogen, der dritte ist eine straff gespannte Sehne. In der Glasbrüstung der Freitreppe leuchten zwei überdimensionierte blaue Pinselstriche. Auch hier zeichnet der eine Strich eine Krümmung, der andere die Gerade. Zwischen diesen zwei einfachen geometrischen Formen, dem Bogen und der Sehne, entsteht eine feine räumliche Spannung.

François Morellet, geboren 1926, lebt und arbeitet in Cholet/Frankreich.

BUILDING 86, ATRIUM AND STAIRCASE | François Morellet, "Bogen, Sehne, Licht" (neon lights, steel cables) and "Bogen, Sehne, Strich" (digital prints, plexiglass, neon lights)

Three red neon tubes hang inside the atrium. Two of them describe a curve, while the third is a tightly stretched cable. On the glass parapet of the exterior stairway glow two oversized blue brushstrokes. Here, too, one stroke is a curve, and the other the straight line. A subtle spatial tension is created between these two simple geometric forms, the curve and the taut cable.

François Morellet, born in 1926, lives and works in Cholet/France.

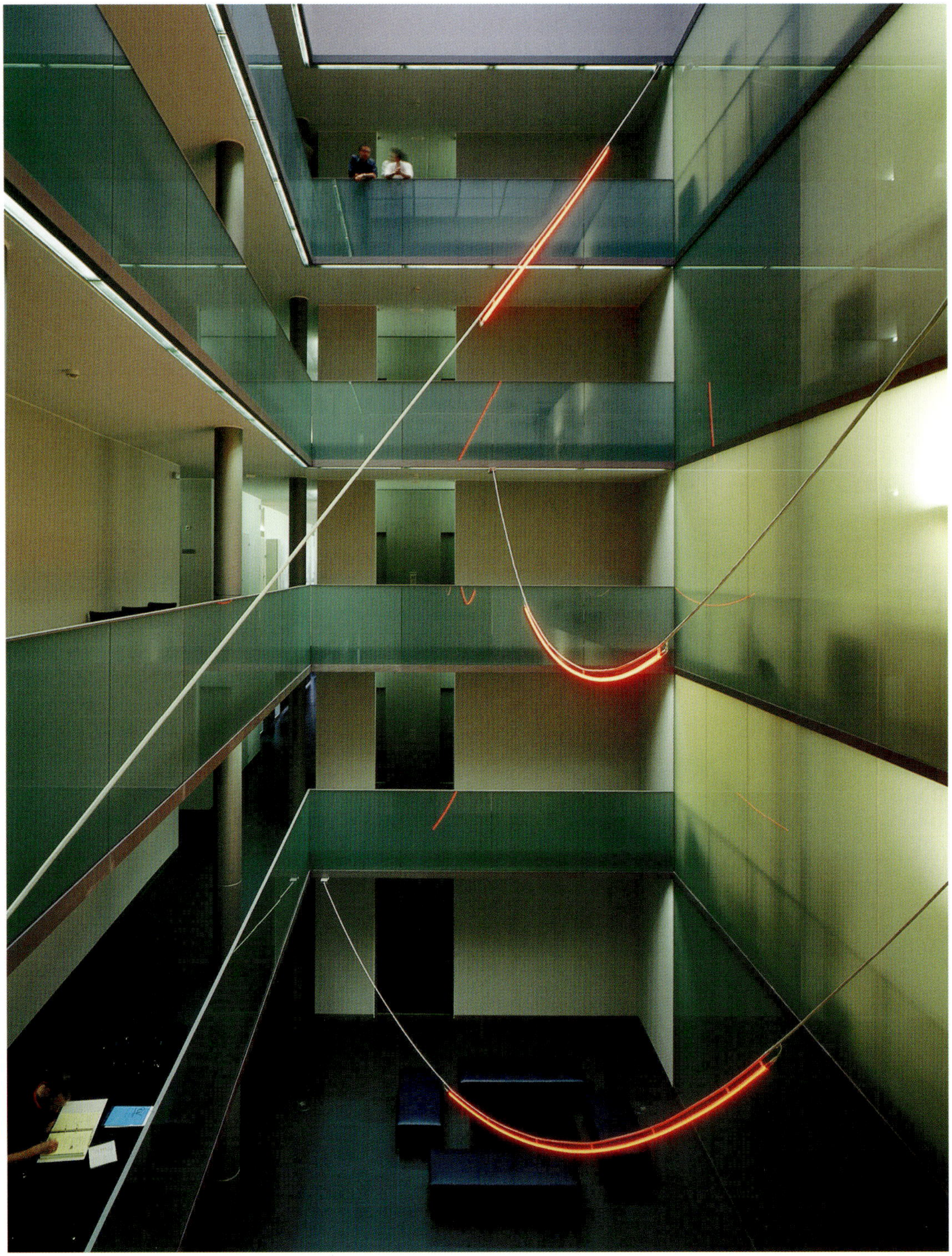

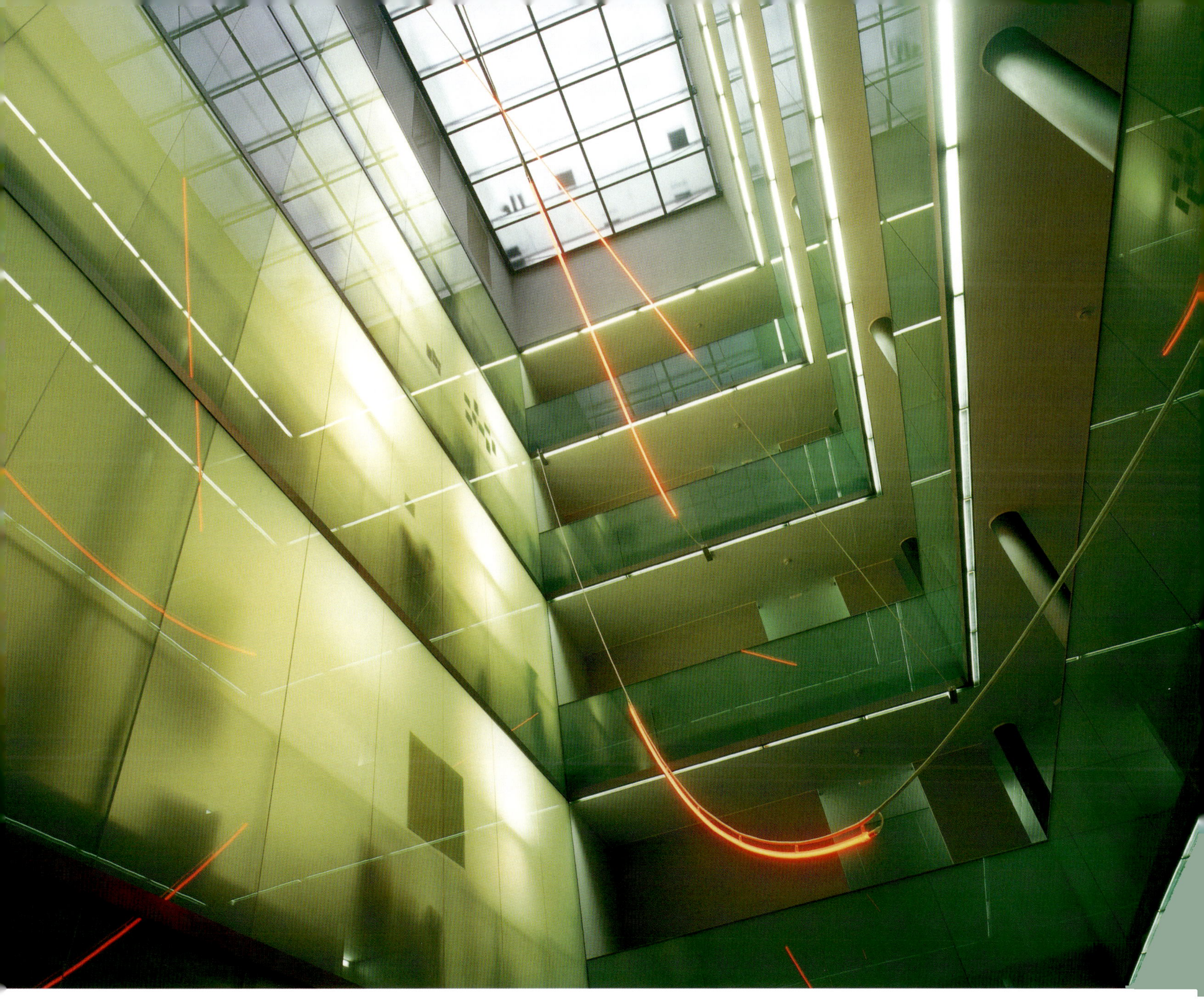

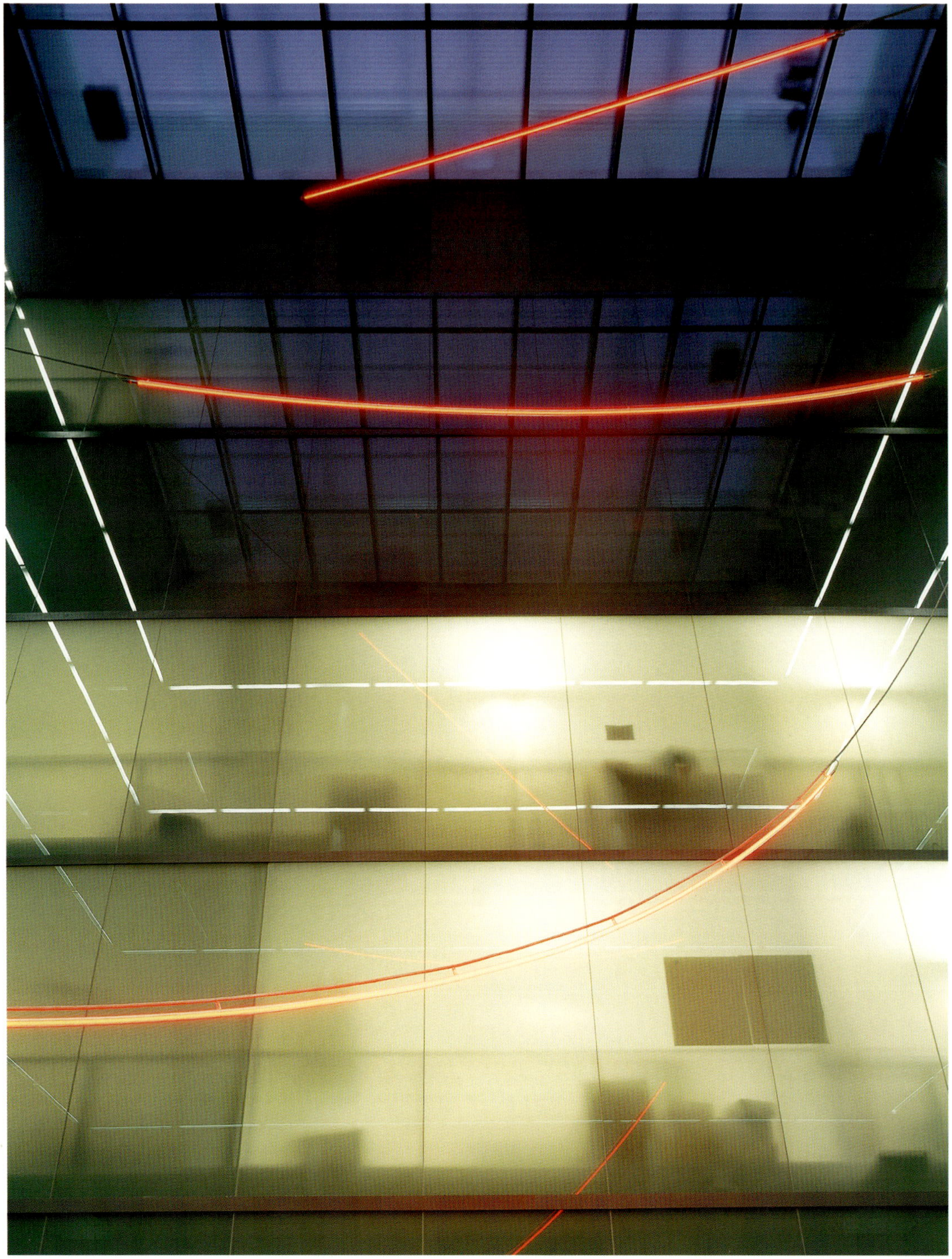

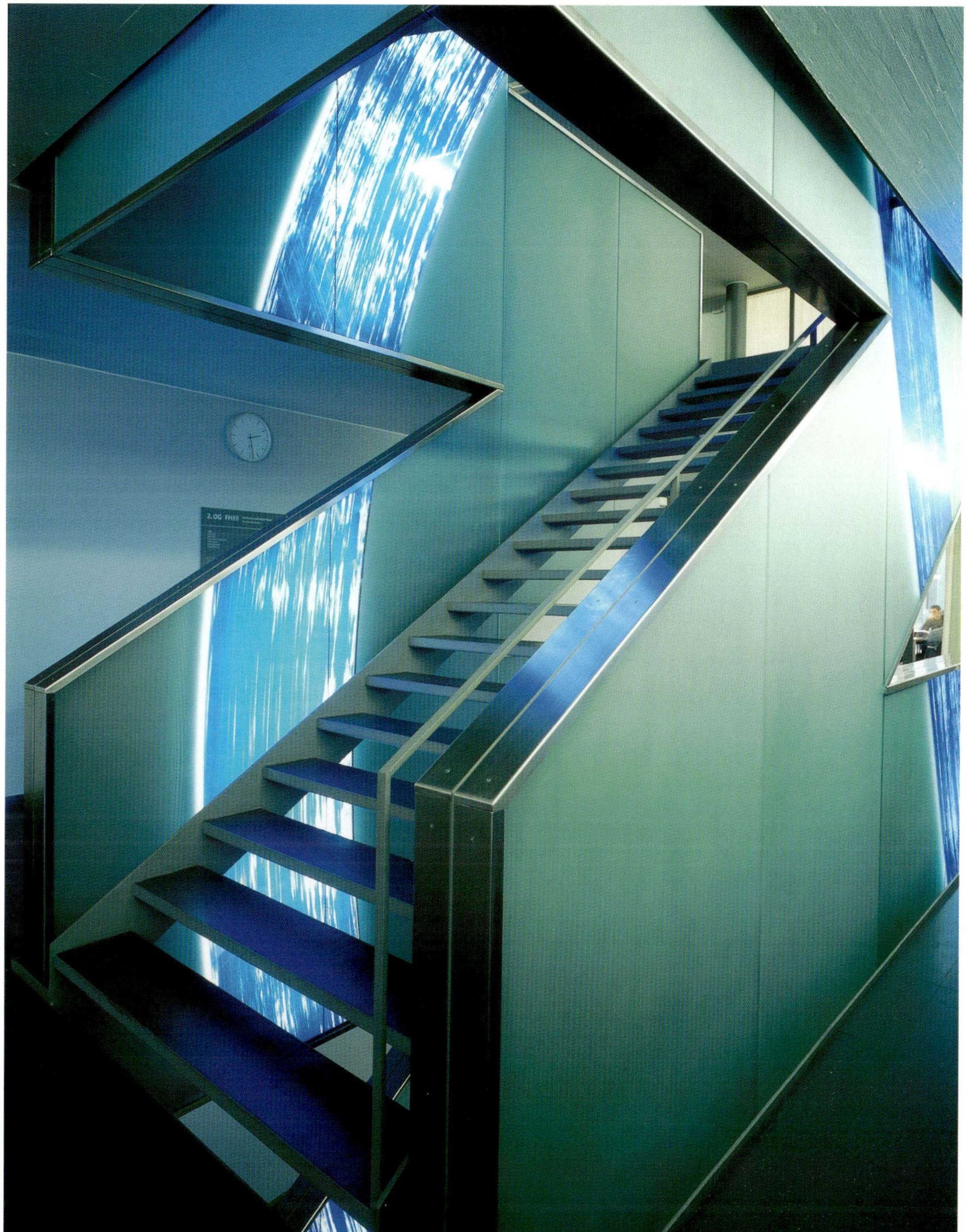

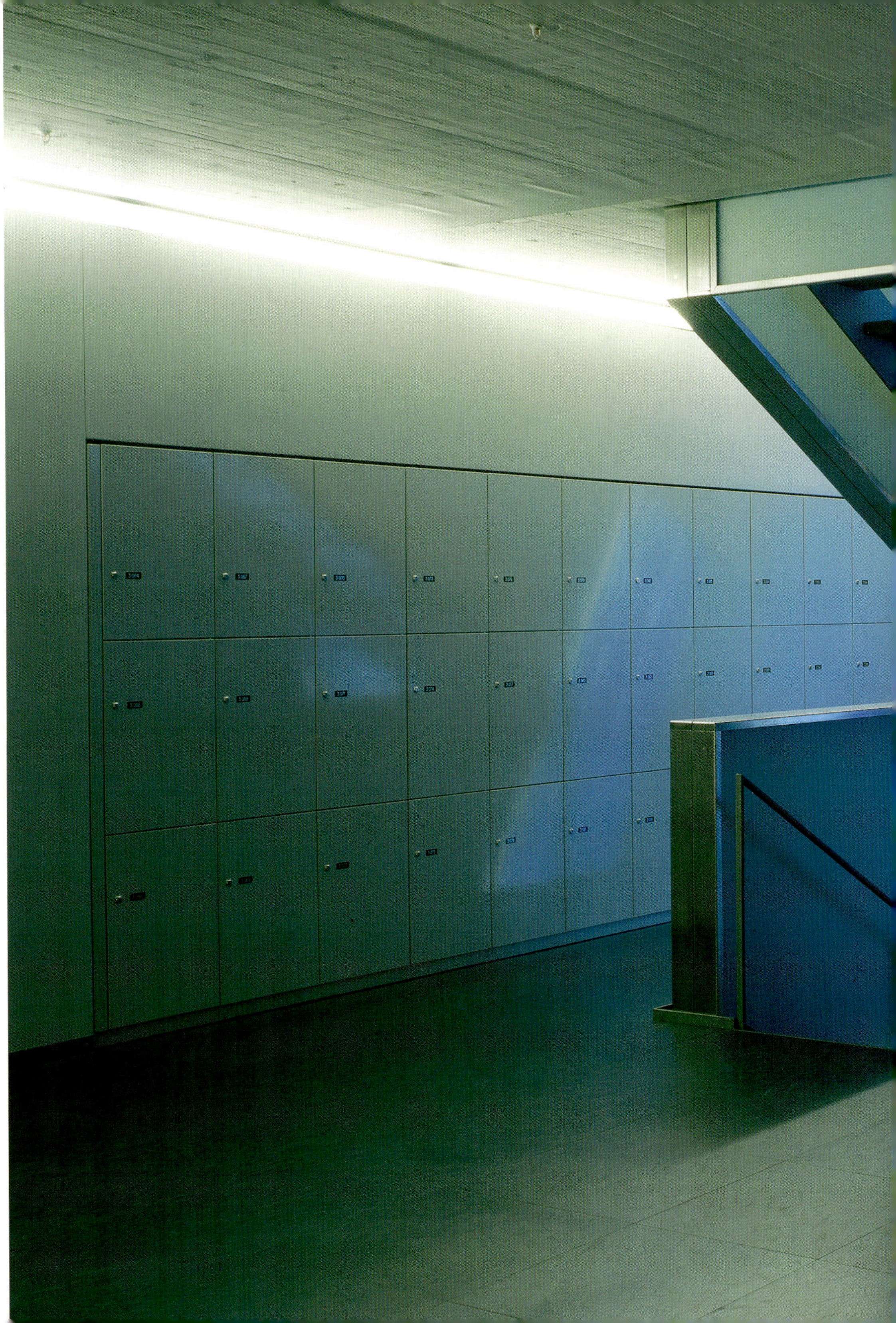

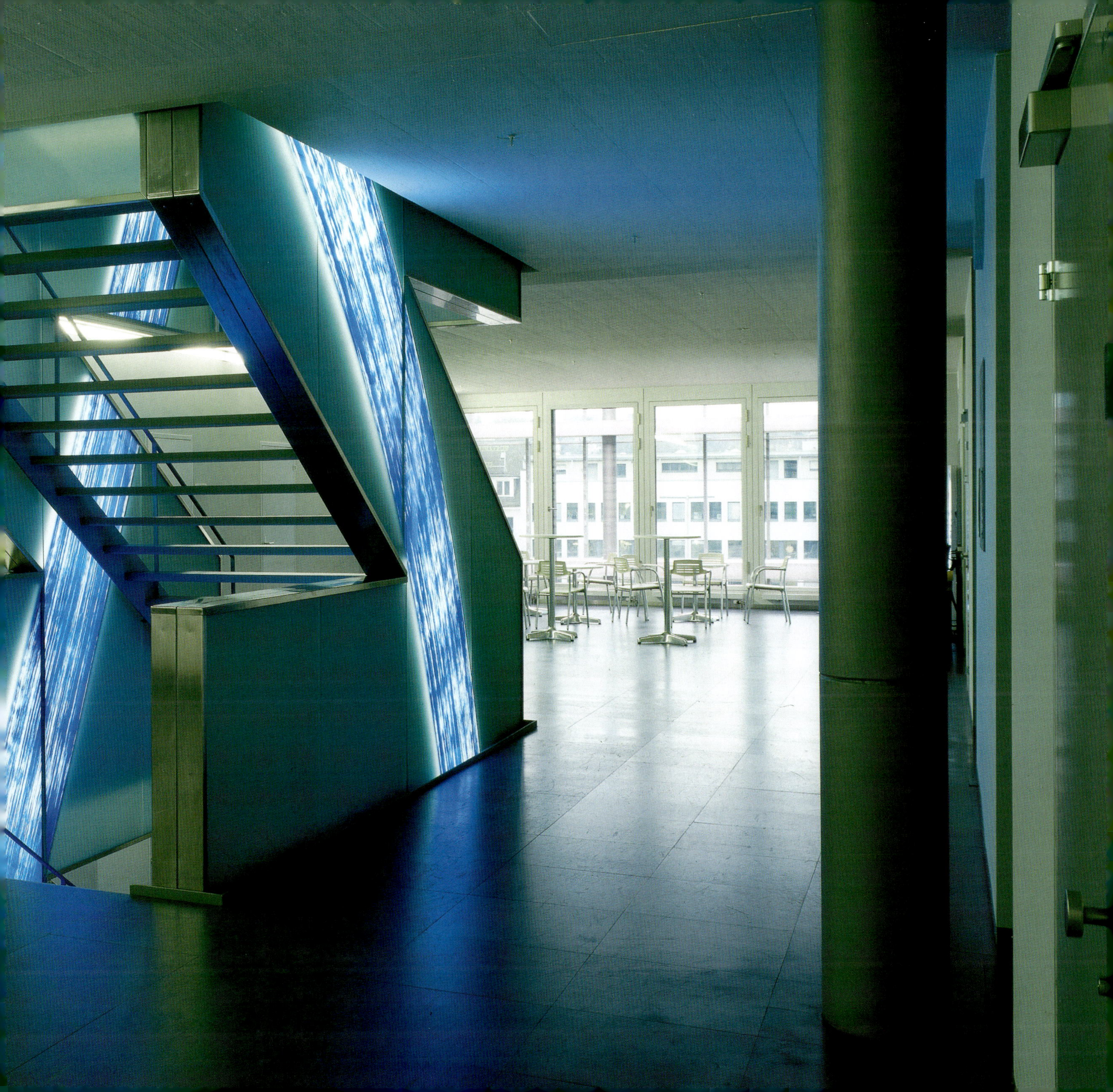

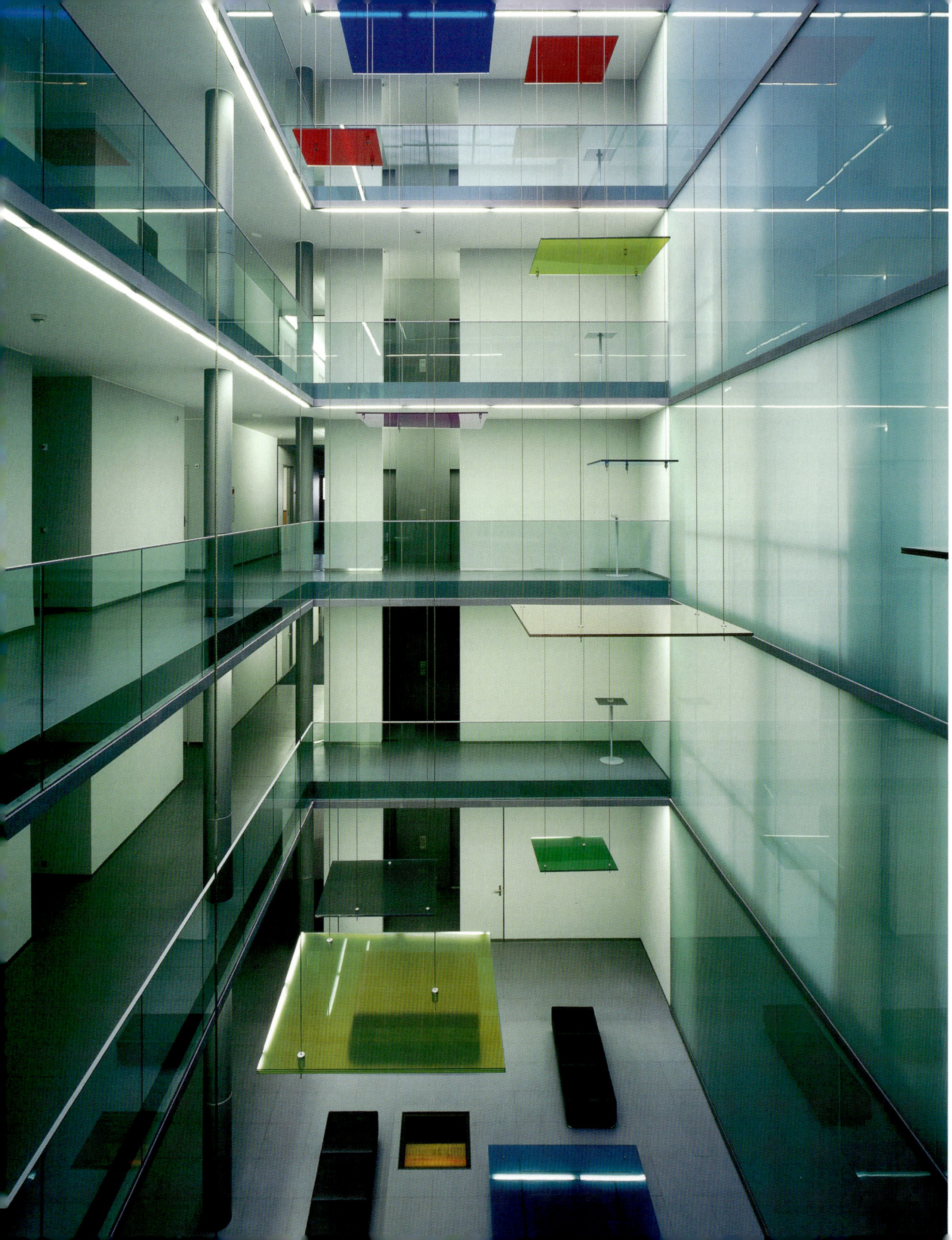

HAUS 88, LICHTHOF | Beat Zoderer, «Räumliches Aquarell»
(20 farbige Glasscheiben im Raum, 20,1 x 13,6 x 6,25 Meter)

An dünnen Stahlseilen hängen verschieden grosse, rechteckige Glasscheiben unterschiedlich tief von der Decke in den Lichthof. Zwischen die Glasscheiben sind Folien geklemmt, daher die Farbe. Obwohl die Arbeit ohne einen Pinselstrich auskommt, vermittelt sie die Wirkung eines Gemäldes – aber nur im Auge des Betrachters. Um diese Wirkung zu erfahren, muss man sich mitten in den Hof stellen und den Kopf in den Nacken legen. Für alle mit weniger Mut empfiehlt es sich, die Scheiben von den Galerien aus zu betrachten. Dann verlieren sie an Gewicht, und die optische Mischung lässt sich auch so wahrnehmen.

Beat Zoderer, geboren 1955, lebt und arbeitet in Wettingen/Schweiz.

BUILDING 88, ATRIUM | Beat Zoderer, "Räumliches Aquarell"
(20 colored glass panels in the space, 20.1 x 13.6 x 6.25 meters)

Rectangular glass panels of various sizes are suspended from the ceiling at different heights on thin steel cables. Colored films are clamped between the glass panels. Without a single brushstroke, the work gives the effect of being a painting – but only in the eye of the observer. To experience the effect, you must stand in the center of the atrium and bend your head all the way back. For those with less courage, viewing the panels from the galleries is recommended. There, some of the impact is lost, but the visual effect can still be perceived.

Beat Zoderer, born in 1955, lives and works in Wettingen/Switzerland.

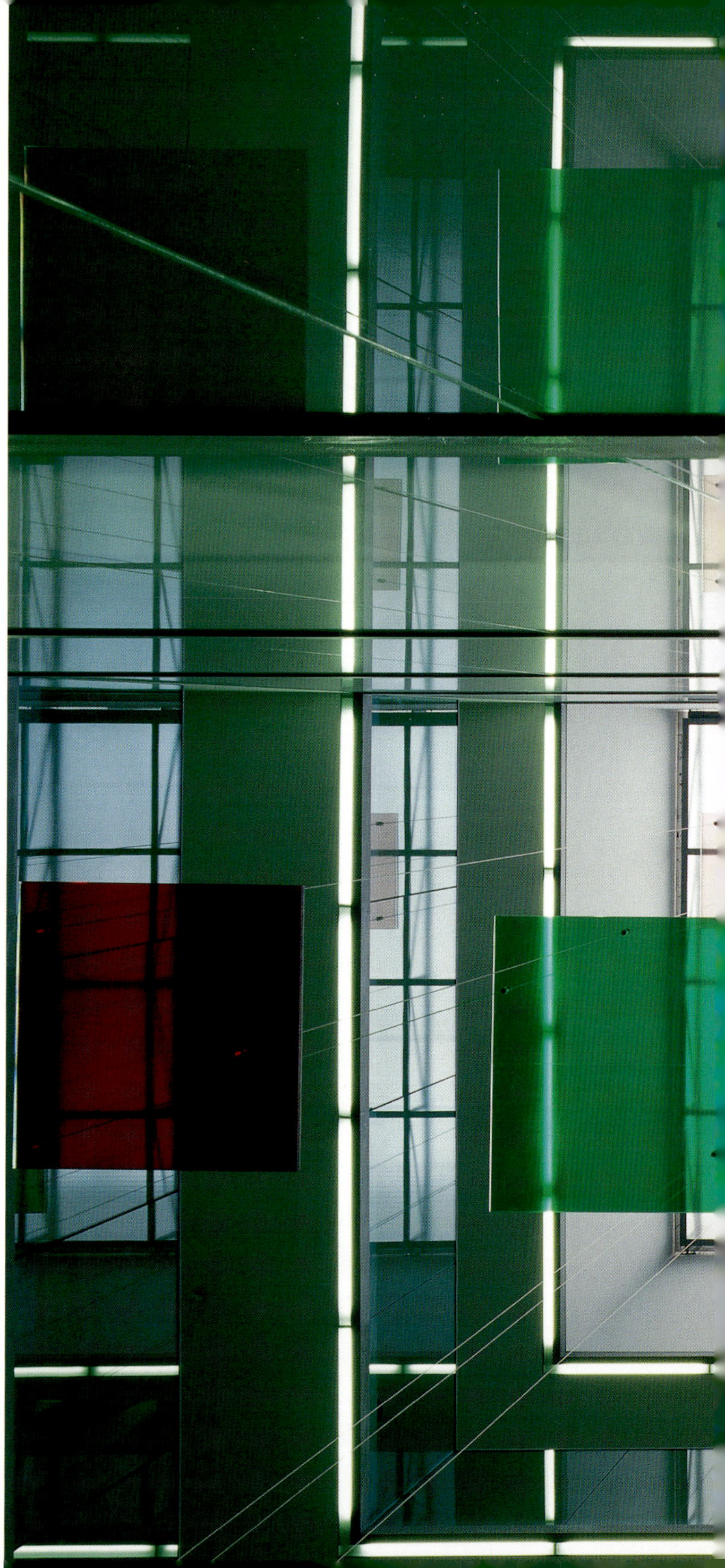

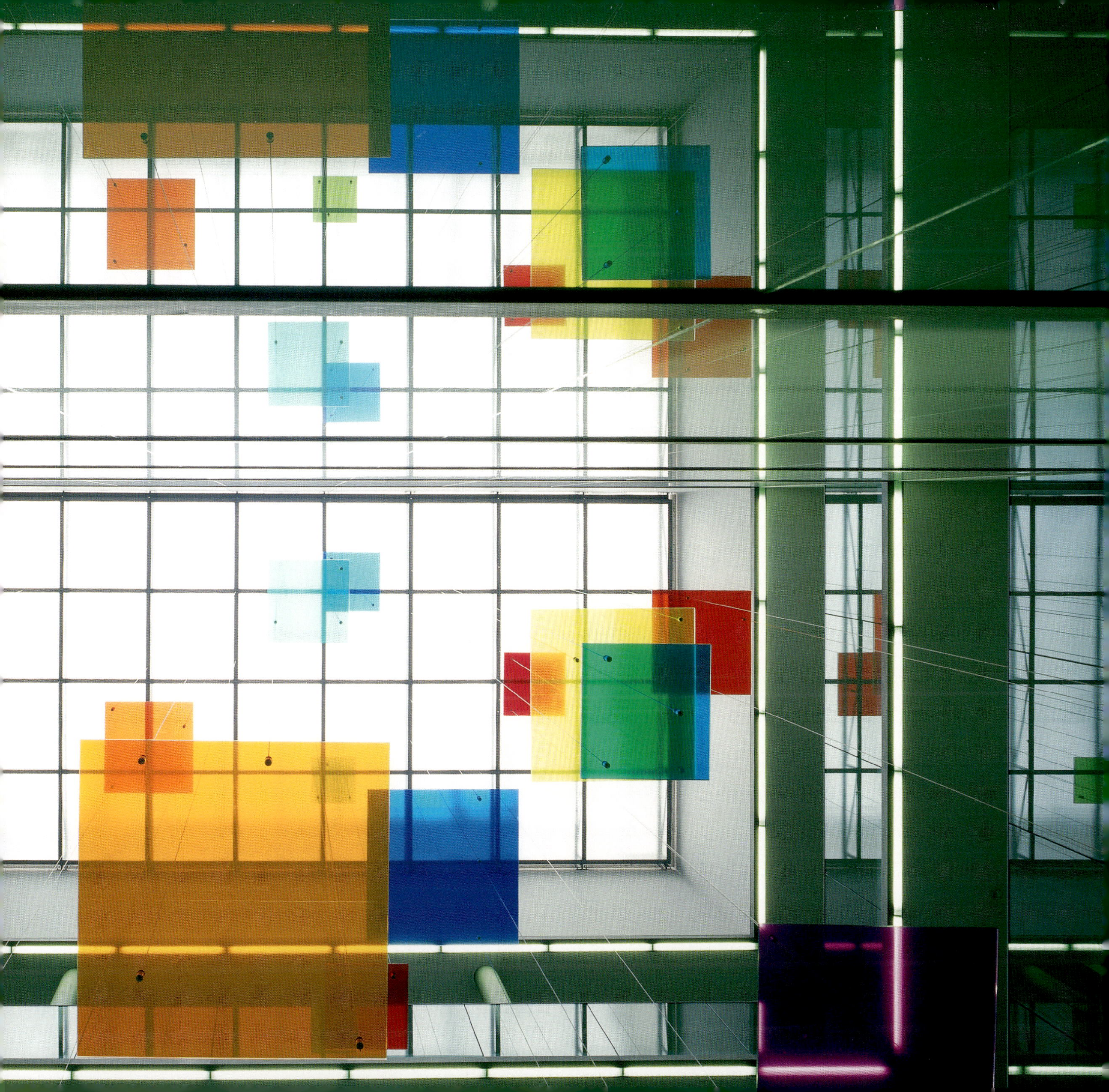

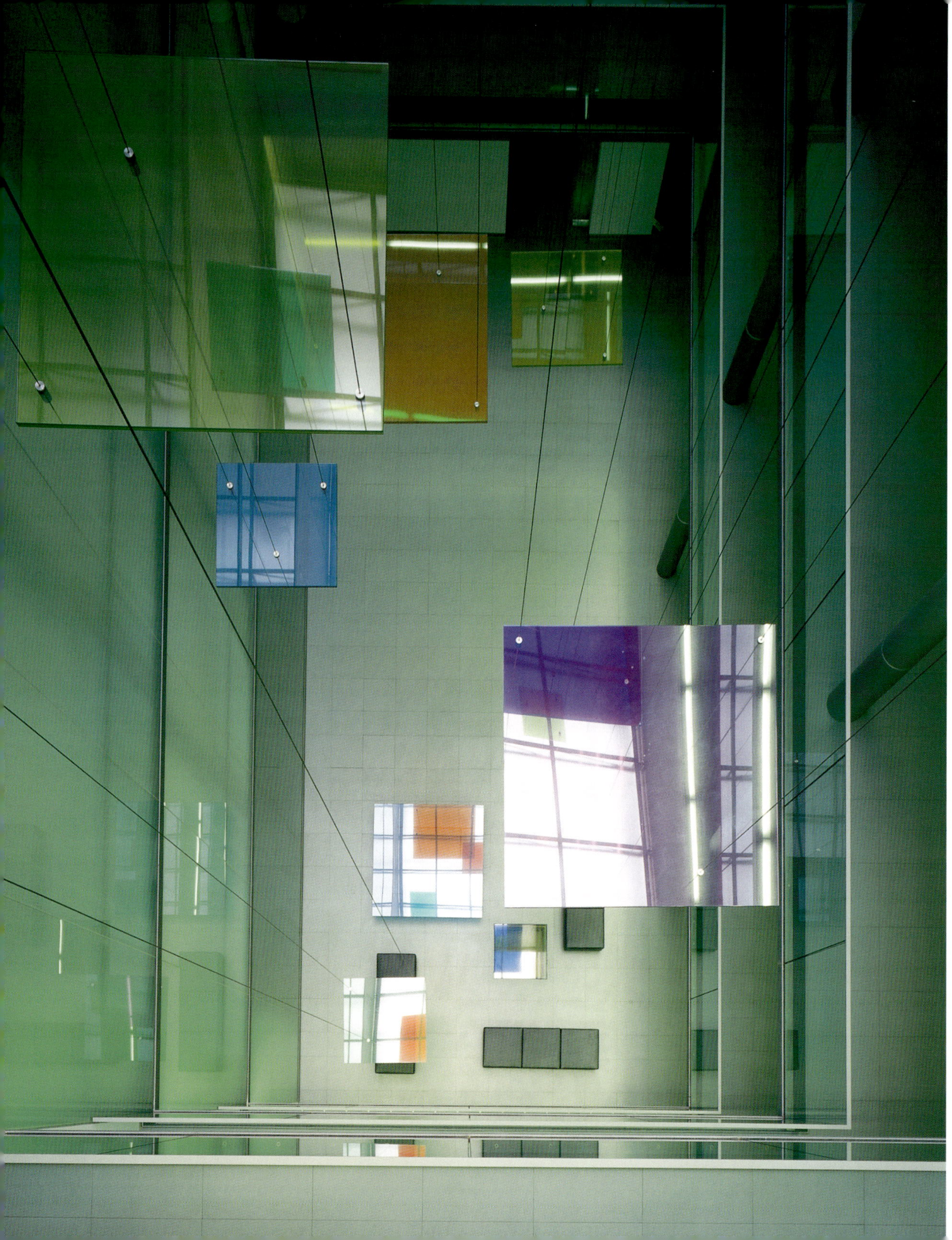

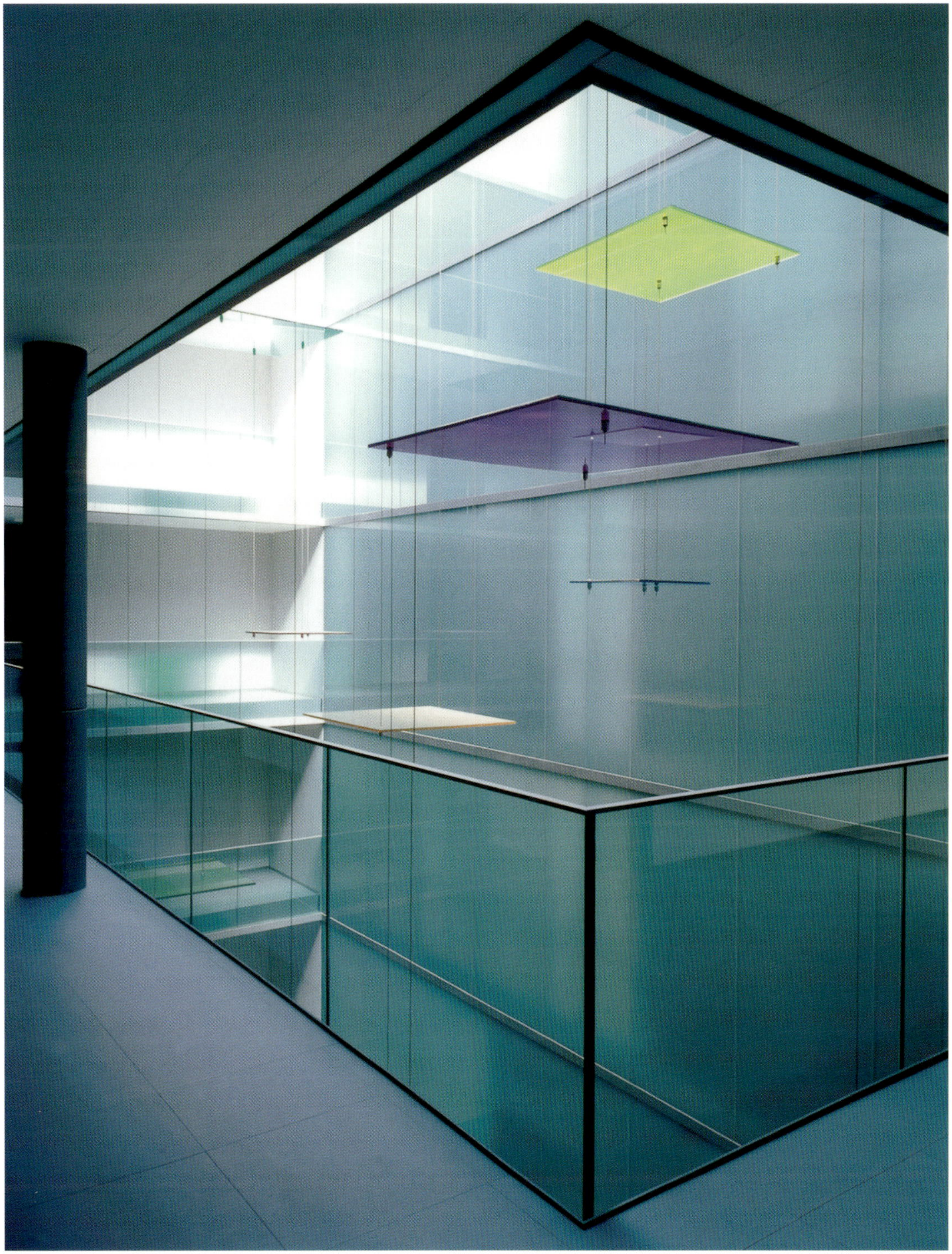

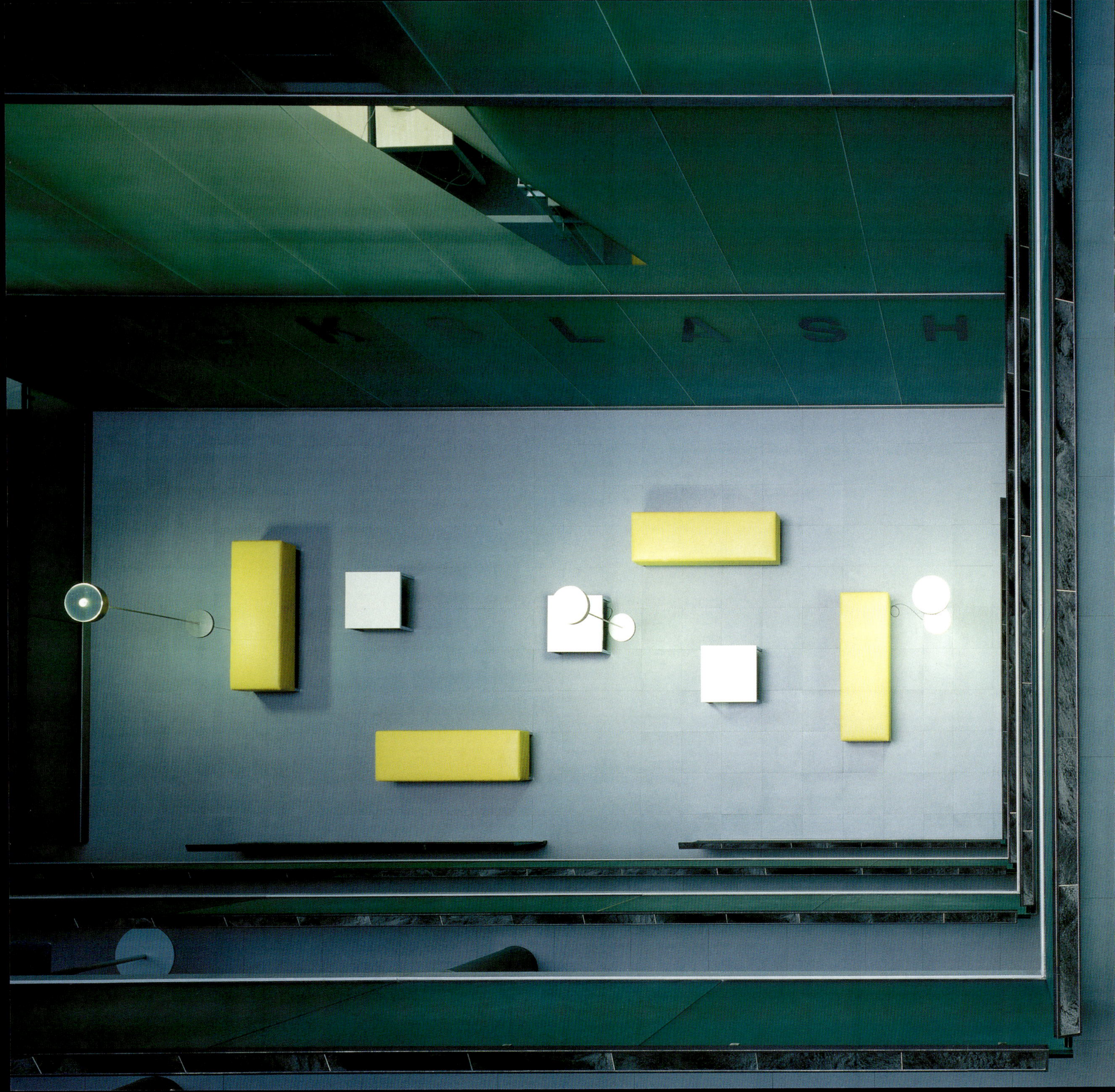

HAUS 90, LICHTHOF | Hans Danuser, «Nah und fern» (Fotografien auf Bromsilberpapier in Eisenfassung, Schrift auf Glas, Licht)

Der Schiefer, auf dem Generationen von Schulkindern das Schreiben lernten, steckt abfotografiert im Handlauf der Balustraden. Der Backslash, ein wichtiges Zeichen in der Programmiersprache, ist überdimensioniert gross direkt vom Computer auf die Glaswand übertragen worden. Der Handlauf mit den mikroskopisch genauen Schieferfotos erinnert in seiner leichten Schräglage an die Panoramatafeln in den Alpen. Das Panorama ist die Glaswand mit dem eingeätzten Backslash. Der (nahe) Schiefer der Wandtafeln und der (ferne) Backslash aus dem Computeralphabet zeigen das Spektrum heute gebräuchlicher Kommunikationsmedien auf.

Hans Danuser, geboren 1953, lebt und arbeitet in Zürich.

BUILDING 90, ATRIUM | Hans Danuser, "Nah und fern" (photographs on bromide silver paper in iron frames, script on glass, light)

Slate, a material that children have been writing and drawing on for generations, was photographed and stuck into the handrail of the parapets. The backslash, an important symbol in computer programming, was transferred directly from the computer to the glass wall as an oversized character. The handrail with its microscopically precise slate photographs and a slight slope reminds us of the panoramic panels found at scenic spots in the Alps. The panorama is the glass wall with the engraved backslash. The (near) slate of the wall panels and the (far) backslash from the computer keyboard illustrate the spectrum of communications media in use today.

Hans Danuser, born in 1953, lives and works in Zurich.

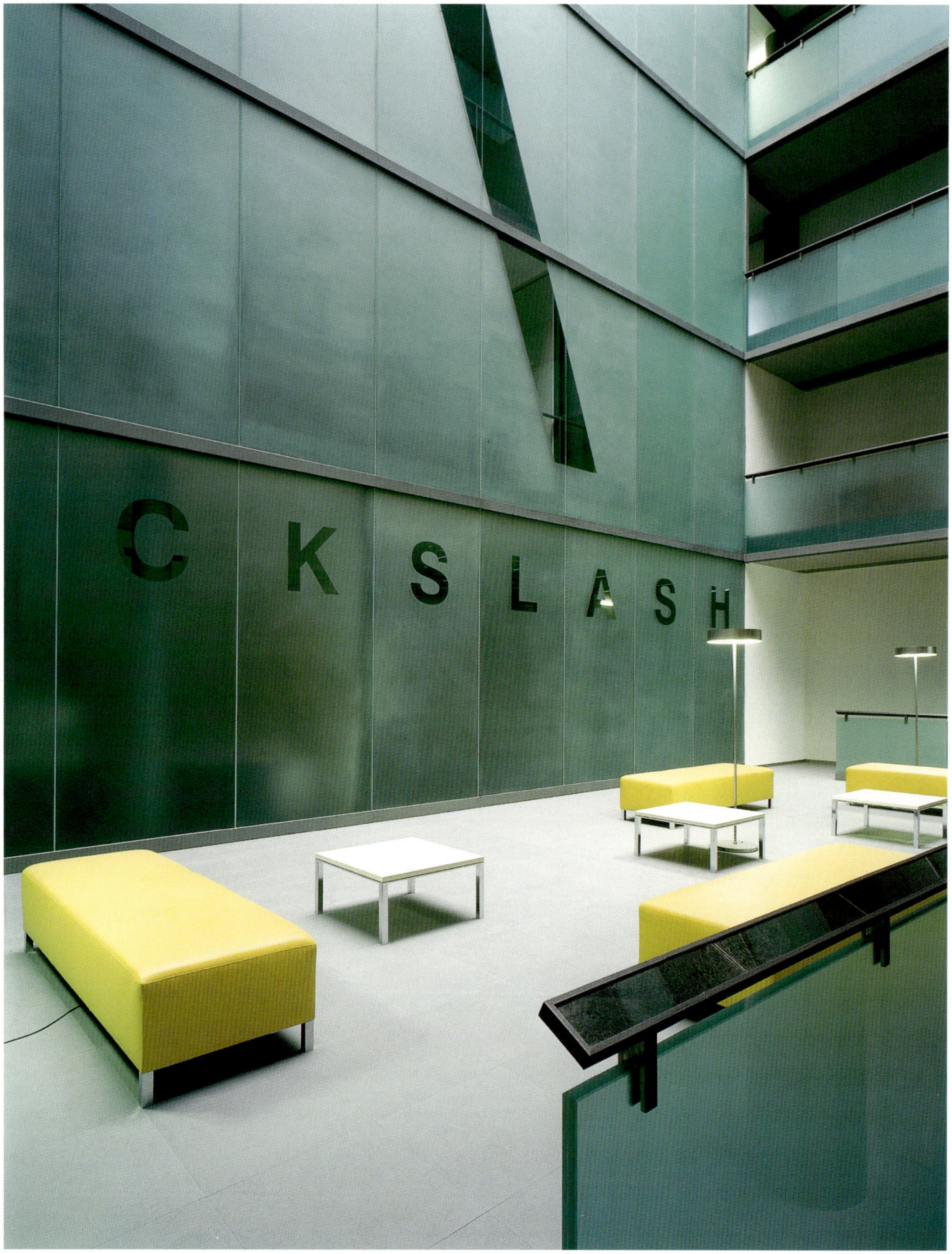
CKSLASH

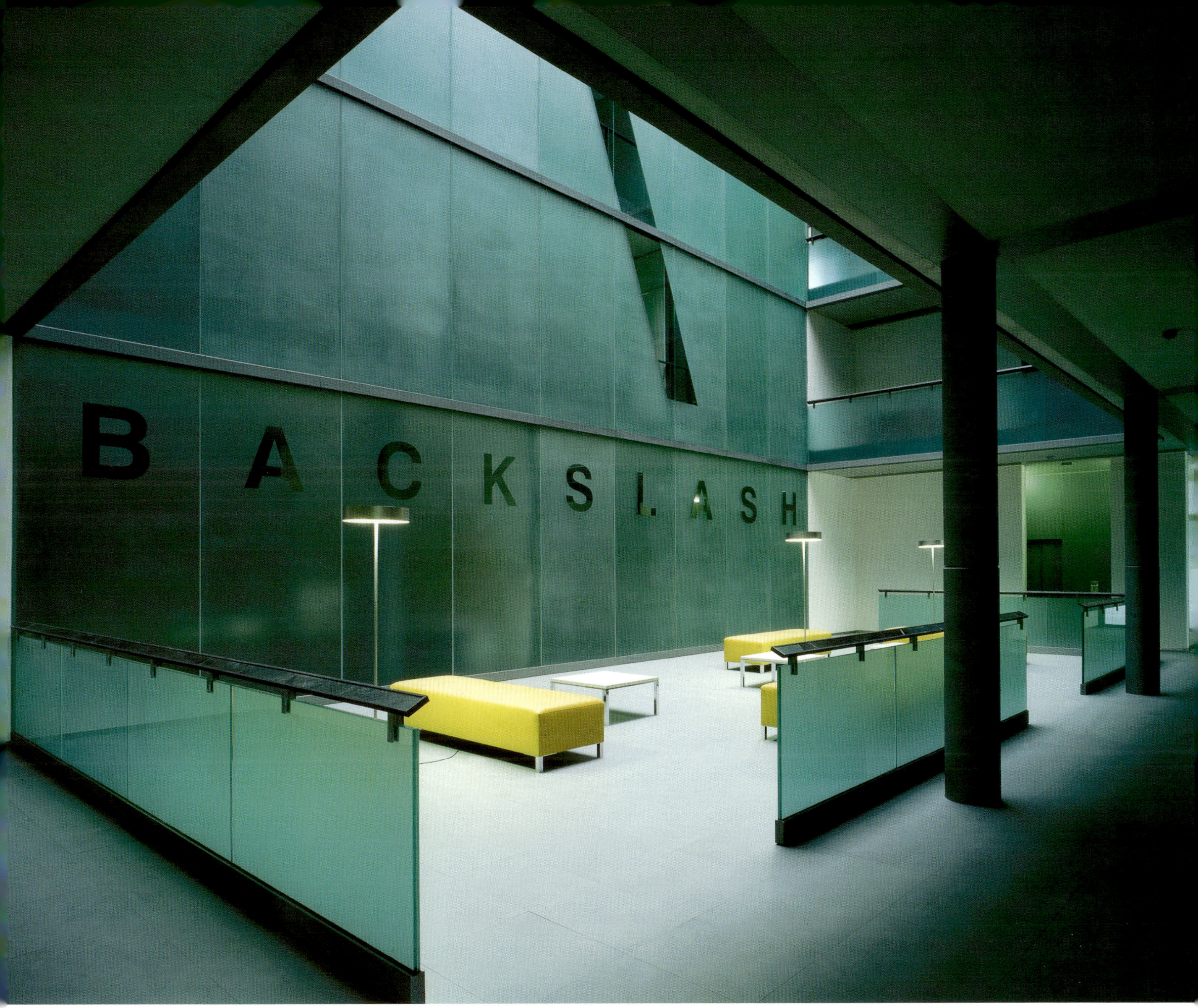
BACKSLASH

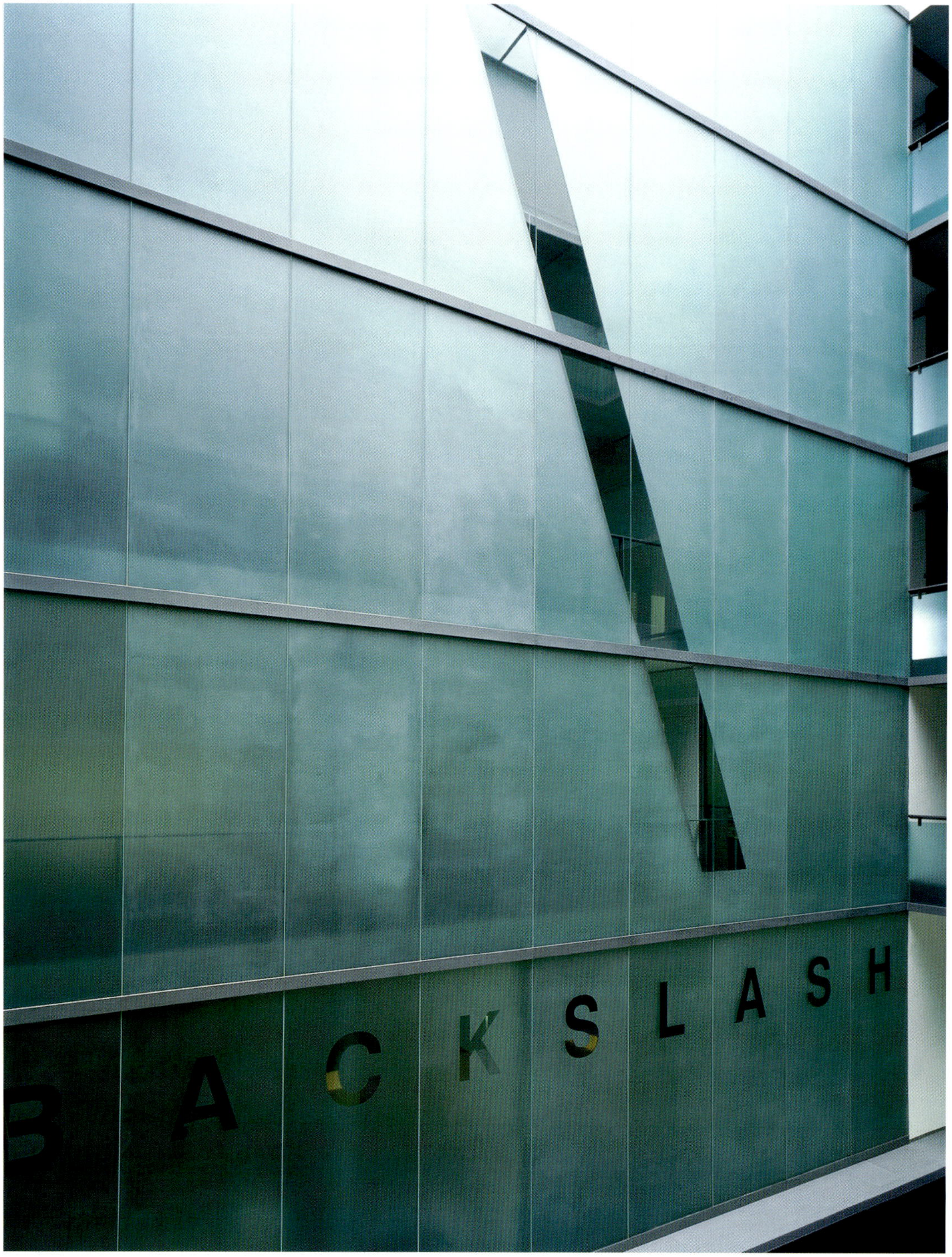
BACKSLASH

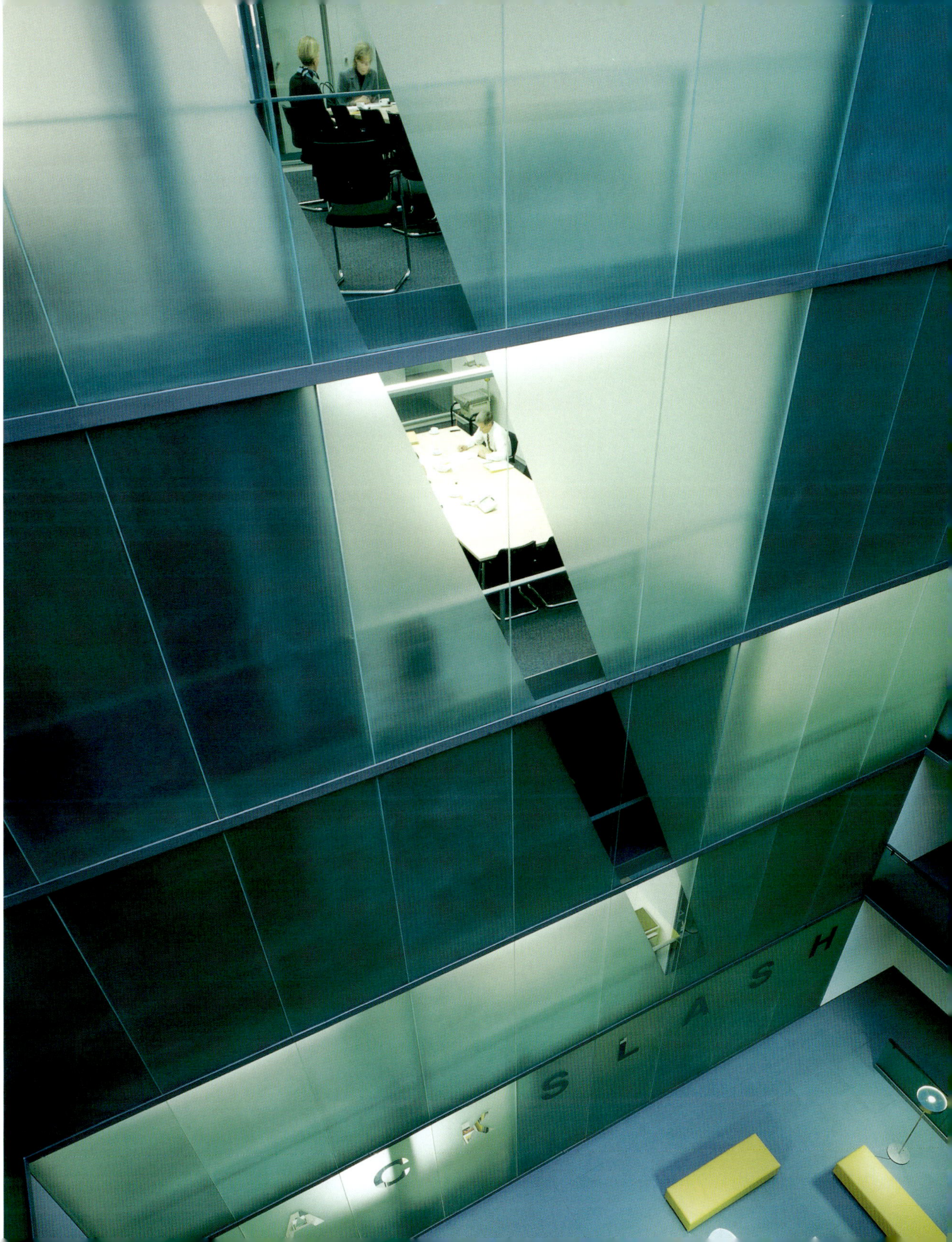
ACKSLASH

VORPLATZ

Der Vorplatz des Peter Merian Hauses wird als Ausstellungsfläche mit wechselnder Bespielung genutzt. Auf dieser Insel im flutenden Verkehr sollen Skulpturen aller Art Akzente setzen und die Kunst, die im Haus in grosser Vielfalt vorhanden ist, nach aussen tragen.

Den Auftakt machte von November 1999 bis Februar 2000 die Arbeit «Urbanes Eis» des Basler Künstlers Eric Hattan. Eric Hattan hat den Vorplatz, der aus vier Platzebenen von jeweils ungefähr 100 m^2 besteht, komplett einesien lassen. In die Eisfelder waren die Signaltafeln von Rogelio Cuenca eingefroren, als Zeichen dafür, dass die Bauarbeiten nun beendet waren. Das Eisfeld wurde professionell betrieben und stand dem Schlittschuh laufenden Publikum zur Verfügung.

Das Folgeprojekt kam von Martin Blum und Haimo Ganz, die auf dem Vorplatz vier riesige Pyramiden aus Altglas aufgeschüttet haben. Es war von März 2000 bis Dezember 2000 zu sehen.

FORECOURT

The forecourt of Peter Merian House is used as an exhibition area. On this island, right in the flow of traffic, sculptures of all kinds will accent and project outwards the wide variety of art existing inside the structure.

The first exhibition was held from November 1999 to February 2000, of the work entitled "Urbanes Eis" by the Basel artist Eric Hattan. Eric Hattan had the forecourt, which consists of four square levels of about 100 m^2 each, completely iced over. The construction signs by Rogelio Cuenca were frozen into the ice fields to indicate that the building work had been concluded. The ice field was professionally managed and was available to the public for skating.

The next project was by Martin Blum and Haimo Ganz, who constructed four huge pyramids of recycled glass on the forecourt. It was on display from March 2000 until December 2000.

1 + 1 = 3 ODER ERFAHRUNGEN MIT «KUNST UND ARCHITEKTUR»

1 + 1 = 3 OR: EXPERIENCES OF "ART AND ARCHITECTURE"

Am Beginn eines Projekts steht immer die Idee und der, der sie hat. Um Künstler und Architekten an einen Tisch und Kunst und Architektur miteinander ins Gespräch zu bringen, sind bei einem Bauvorhaben viele Voraussetzungen vonnöten, unverzichtbar sind folgende: Durchhaltevermögen. Sturheit. Überzeugung. Leidenschaft. Man kann es nennen, wie man will: Am Anfang eines solchen Projekts steht der, der es umsetzen will, also der Architekt mit seiner starken Liebe zur Kunst und zu denen, die sie dem Leben abringen, den zeitgenössischen Künstlerinnen und Künstlern. Hans Zwimpfer war und ist davon überzeugt, dass aus der Verbindung von Kunst und Architektur etwas Drittes entstehen kann, nicht Kunst am Bau, nicht Kunst als Dekoration der Architektur, sondern etwas Neues, etwas So-noch-nie-Dagewesenes, das die Architektur verändert und sich für die Benutzer in einem Plus an Lebensqualität niederschlägt. Für diesen Mehrwert gibt es kein Einheitsrezept. Beim Peter Merian Haus haben sich jedoch die folgenden Punkte als die wichtigsten erwiesen:

Der Architekt musste für seinen Traum vom Einbezug der Kunst zunächst ein Konzept entwickeln. Er musste sich darüber klar werden, was er von der Kunst im Rahmen dieses Bauprojekts erwartete. Das war keine Aufgabe, die er alleine lösen konnte. Deswegen hat er sich von Fachleuten für zeitgenössische Kunst beraten lassen. Aus diesen Gesprächen resultierten wichtige Anregungen und Klärungen. Die Qualität und Unabhängigkeit der Berater war wichtig, unbestritten blieb jedoch zu jedem Zeitpunkt, dass die Gesamtverantwortung für das Projekt vollumfänglich beim Architekten lag. Dies bedeutete auch, dass keine wesentlichen Entscheidungen wie zum Beispiel die Auswahl der Künstlerinnen und Künstler an Dritte delegiert wurden.

In der Verantwortung des Projektleiters lag es ferner auch, dafür zu sorgen, dass der Einbezug der Kunst finanzierbar war. Aus diesem Grund mussten die Aufwendungen für die Kunst schon im ersten Kostenvoranschlag budgetiert werden. Sie sind Teil des urbanistischen

A project always starts with the idea and the person who originally had it. To bring artists and architects together at one table, and to initiate dialog between art and architecture in a building project, many conditions are necessary, notably: stamina, stubbornness, conviction, passion. Call it what you will: at the beginning of such a project is the person who really wants to realize it, the architect with a strong love of art, as well as those who wring art from life – the contemporary artists. Hans Zwimpfer remains convinced that a third element can emerge from the combination of art and architecture: not just art in the building, as a decoration of architecture, but something new and unprecedented which changes architecture and raises the quality of life for its users. There is no general recipe for this added value. In the case of Peter Merian House, however, the following aspects turned out to be the most important.

For his dream of artistic integration, the architect first had to develop a clear concept. He needed to clarify for himself what he expected from the art in this building project. This was not a task he could accomplish alone. He therefore consulted experts on contemporary art. These talks produced important suggestions and clarifications. While the quality and independence of the consultants was important, there is no doubt that at every stage the architect carried the full overall responsibility for the project. This also meant that no essential decisions, such as the selection of the artists, were delegated to third parties.

It was part of the project manager's responsibilities to ensure that the integration of the art could be financed. For this reason, the cost of the art had to be included in the proposed budget. The cost forms part of the urban concept developed for a new building and thus were defined from the outset. As always when it comes to money, a great deal of persuasion was necessary. Clients, investors and entrepreneurs were not as convinced as the architect of the necessity of the art. It is to his credit that he found acceptance and the necessary funding for "Art and Architecture".

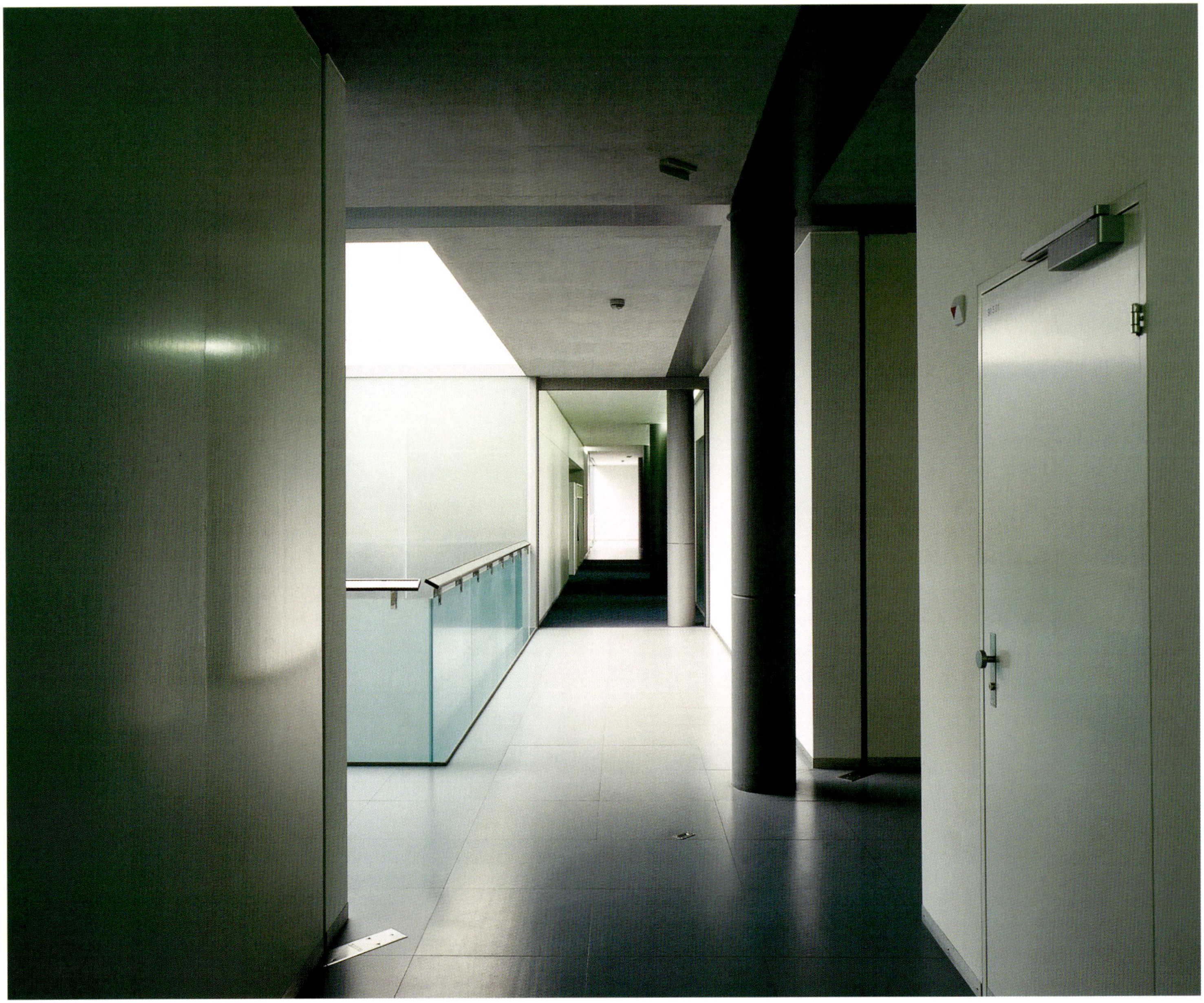

Konzepts, das für einen Neubau entwickelt wird, und insofern von Anfang an definiert. Wie immer, wenn es ums Geld geht, war hier viel Überzeugungsarbeit nötig. Bauherren, Investoren, Unternehmer waren nicht im selben Mass von der Notwendigkeit der Kunst überzeugt wie der Architekt. Es ist sein Verdienst, für «Kunst und Architektur» Akzeptanz und die nötigen finanziellen Mittel gefunden zu haben.

Nachdem die Rahmenbedingungen geschaffen waren, ging es um die Auswahl der beteiligten Künstlerinnen und Künstler. Auch hier war der Architekt auf den Rat von Fachleuten angewiesen. Rückblickend lässt sich festhalten, dass eine Zusammenarbeit mit den Künstlern dann möglich wurde, wenn diese über eine so ausgereifte Bildsprache verfügten, dass sie es mit der Dimension des Peter Merian Hauses aufnehmen konnten. Die Künstler mussten bereit sein, einerseits die Trägheit architektonischer Prozesse zu ertragen, andererseits die Architekten als Gesprächspartner auch in konzeptuellen und ästhetischen Fragen ernst zu nehmen. Drittens mussten sie selbst professionell organisiert sein, um über mehrere Jahre hinweg an einem Projekt arbeiten zu können.

Überhaupt erwies sich der Terminplan als zentraler Punkt: Bei einem Projekt wie dem Peter Merian Haus konnte man höchstens zu spät dran sein, niemals zu früh. Da die Künstlerinnen und Künstler mit ihren Arbeiten die Architektur nicht schmücken, sondern mitprägen sollten, wurden sie sehr früh in den Prozess der Planung einbezogen. Dadurch hatte man Zeit, aufeinander zuzugehen, Vorurteile abzubauen, sich kennenzulernen. Und die Arbeiten der Künstler konnten fugenlos in die Architektur eingepasst werden.

Die Zusammenarbeit mit den Künstlerinnen und Künstlern war von Diskussionen, rauchenden Köpfen, mancher Auseinandersetzung, aber auch von eigentlichen Sternstunden der Inspiration gekennzeichnet. Hans Zwimpfer war es dabei stets ein Anliegen, diesen Prozess in einem offenen und konstruktiven Klima durchzuführen. Bei gemeinsa-

After the framework conditions had been established, attention turned towards the selection of the participating artists. Here, too, the architect was dependent on expert advice. In retrospect it can be seen that cooperation with the artists became possible if they provided a symbolic language that was mature enough to match the dimensions of Peter Merian House. The artists had to be willing both to endure the inertia of the architectural process, and to take the architects seriously as partners in the discussion of conceptual and aesthetic issues. They also had to be professionally well-organized enough to work on a project over several years.

The schedule turned out to be a central issue: in a project like Peter Merian House, you could be too late, but never too early. Since the artists' work was intended not to decorate but to influence the architecture, it was integrated into the planning process early on. There was therefore time to make contact, to remove prejudices and to get to know each other. And the artists' work could be seamlessly integrated into the architecture.

The collaboration with the artists was marked by discussion, frank exchanges and a few disagreements, but also moments of genuine inspiration. Hans Zwimpfer was always concerned to realize this process in an open and constructive climate. More than one problem was solved over lunches or dinners, and the various openings that took place before the project ended brought public attention and success. The friendly atmosphere was as important to the fruitfulness of the collaboration as the serious work of all the participants.

"Art and Architecture" at Peter Merian House was a risk, an open-ended adventure. All who took part can be proud of its happy ending. The thoughts of Hans Zwimpfer have, in the meantime, moved on: "Art and Architecture" will continue in Jacob Burckhardt House and, it is hoped, imitated in diverse ways in other architects' projects!

men Mittag- und Abendessen konnte mehr als ein Problem ausgeräumt werden, und die verschiedenen Vernissagen, die schon vor Abschluss des Projekts stattfanden, haben ihm Aufmerksamkeit verschafft und für Erfolgserlebnisse gesorgt. Die freundschaftliche Atmosphäre war für das Gelingen ebenso wichtig wie die seriöse Arbeit, die von allen Beteiligten geleistet wurde.

«Kunst und Architektur» am Peter Merian Haus war ein Wagnis, ein Abenteuer mit offenem Ausgang. Auf sein glückliches Ende können alle Beteiligten stolz sein. Die Gedanken von Hans Zwimpfer sind indes schon einen Schritt weiter: Was man gemeinsam am Peter Merian Haus erreicht hat, soll kein einmaliger Erfolg bleiben. «Kunst und Architektur» wird am Jacob Burckhardt Haus seine Fortführung und in den Projekten anderer Architekten und Architektinnen hoffentlich vielfältige Nachahmung finden!

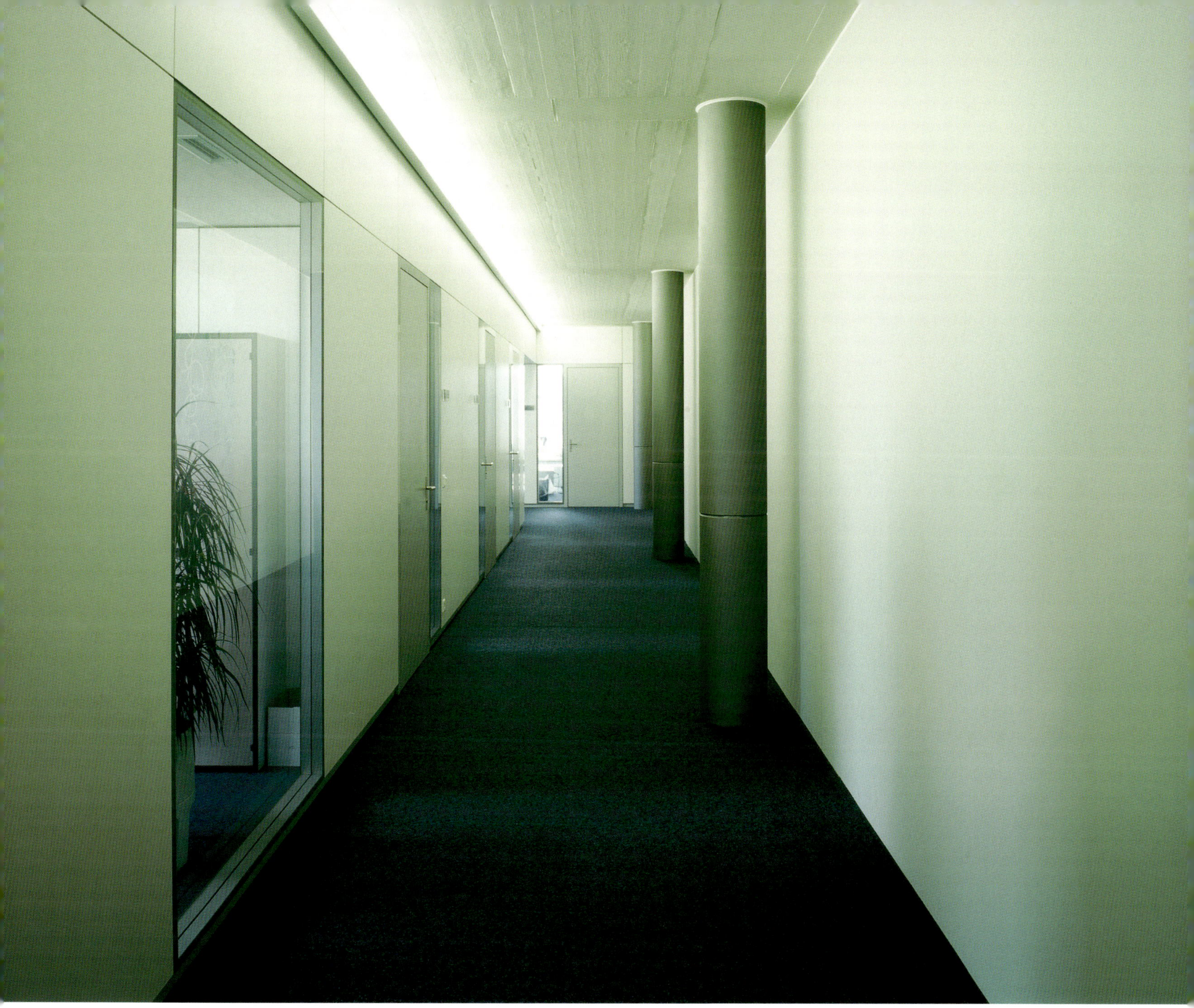

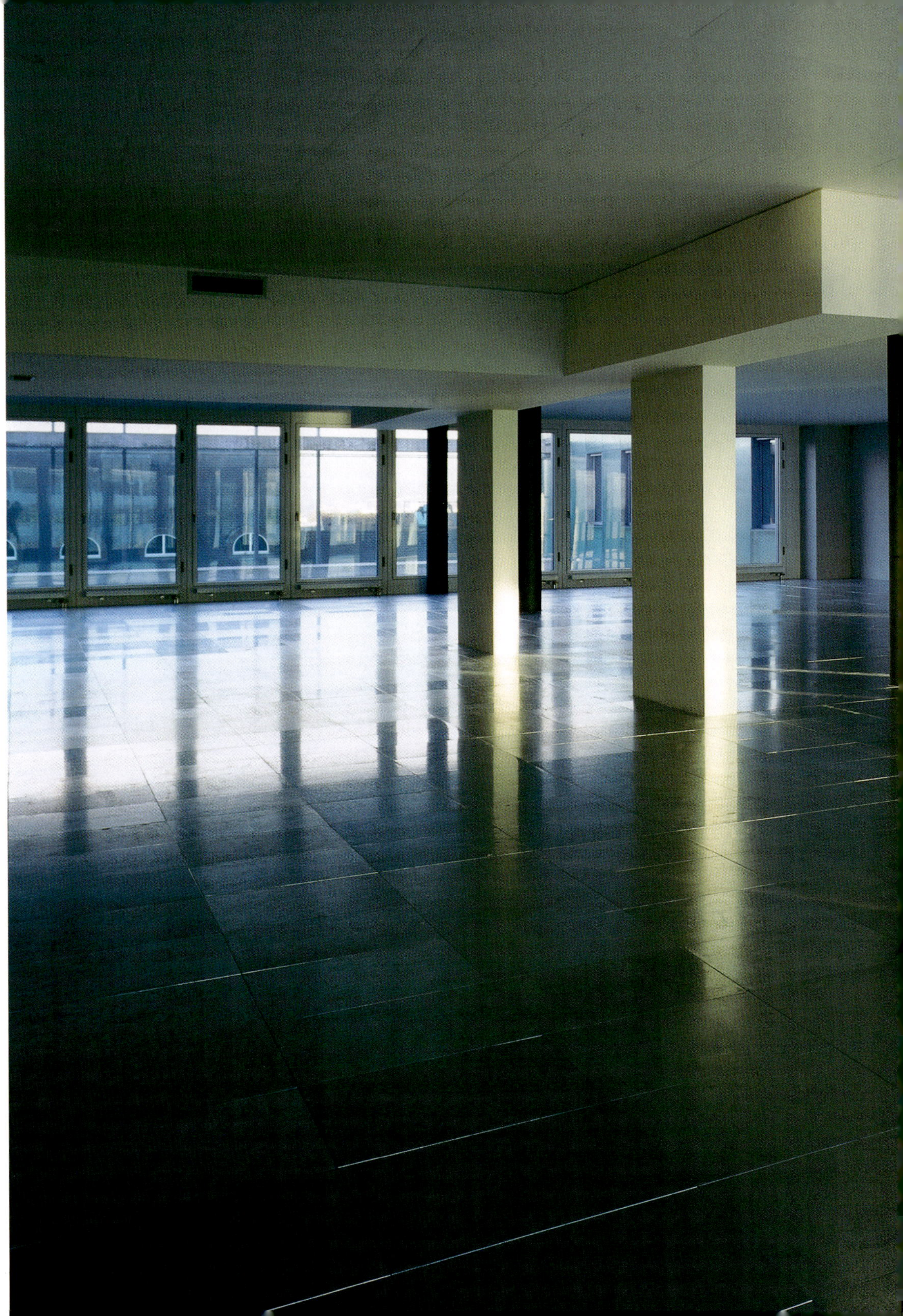

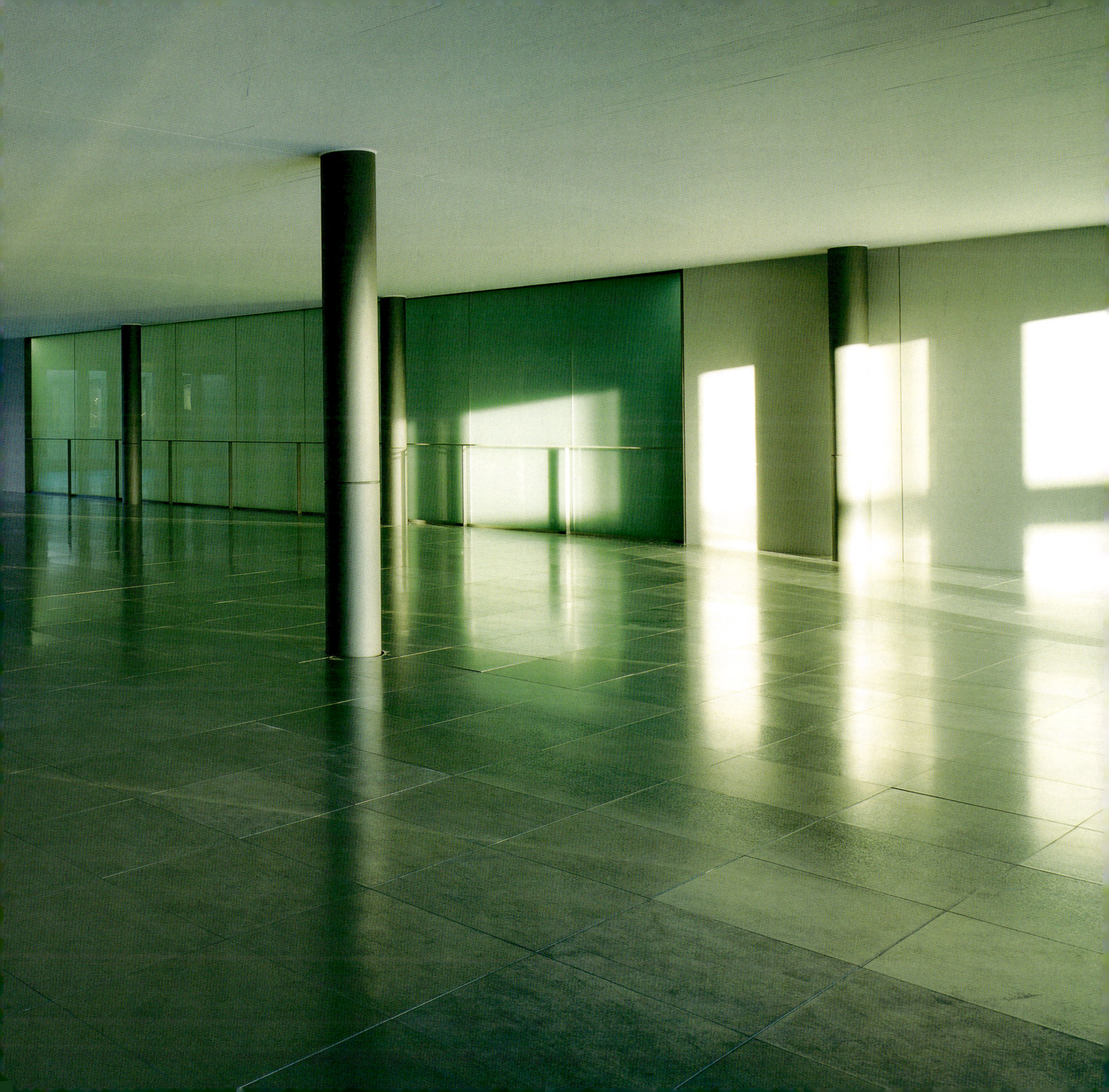

PLANUNGS- UND BAUGESCHICHTE

Als das Peter Merian Haus am 21. September 2000 eingeweiht wurde, blickte es bereits auf eine 14 Jahre währende, wechselhafte Geschichte zurück. Ursprünglich als Postgebäude mit Postbahnhof geplant, wird es nun überwiegend privatwirtschaftlich genutzt. Wie kam es zu diesem veränderten Verwendungszweck schon vor der Einweihung?

In den frühen achtziger Jahren setzen sich in Basel verschiedene Interessengruppen an einen Tisch, um Zukunftsperspektiven für das Gebiet um den Basler Bahnhof SBB (der Bahnhof der Schweizerischen Bundesbahnen) zu erarbeiten. Es entsteht ein Projekt, das als Basler Masterplan in die Geschichte eingehen wird. Sein Anliegen ist der Ausbau der Stadt innerhalb der Stadtgrenzen. 1986 meldet sich die Projektgruppe Bahnhof Ost in Sachen Masterplan zu Wort. Ihre treibende Kraft ist der Architekt Hans Zwimpfer. Diese Gruppe unterbreitet folgenden Vorschlag: Auf dem Ostteil des Masterplangebiets soll ein neuer, unterirdischer Postbahnhof entstehen. Über dem Postbahnhof sollen Betriebs-, Dienstleistungs- und Bürobauten errichtet werden. Die Projektgruppe erstellt eine Nutzungsstudie. Sowohl PTT (heute Die Post) wie SBB (Schweizerische Bundesbahnen) zeigen sich interessiert. 1987 wird die Immobiliengesellschaft Bahnhof Ost AG (I.B.O.) gegründet. Ihre Aufgabe ist die Promotion und Vermarktung des Projekts Bahnhof Ost. 1988 werden die Generalplanerverträge abgeschlossen. Die Grundsteine zur Realisierung des Projekts Bahnhof Ost sind gelegt. Im selben Jahr findet die Einzonung des Baugeländes statt. 1989 und 1990 wird die statische Konstruktion des Neubaus festgelegt. Über die kubische Ausgestaltung wird diskutiert.

1991 befindet sich die Schweizer Wirtschaft in der Rezession. Die Post stellt nun die Notwendigkeit eines neuen Postbahnhofs in Basel in Frage. Die Anzahl der Gleise wird von zehn auf sechs reduziert. Auch die Wertquoten zwischen Post und I.B.O. werden neu verteilt. Die Post schraubt ihren Anteil von 80 auf 70 Prozent herunter, die I.B.O. ihren von 20 auf 30 Prozent herauf.

PLANNING AND BUILDING HISTORY

When Peter Merian House was opened on September 21, 2000 it could already look back on a 14-year history full of change. Originally planned as a post office building with a postal station, it is now mainly used by private companies. How did this change of purpose come about even before the opening?

During the early 1980s, various special interest groups in Basel came together to consider future plans for the area surrounding the Basel SBB station. A project emerged that would enter the history books as the Basel master plan. Its primary concern was the expansion of the city within the city limits. In 1986, the Project Group Bahnhof Ost (East Station) took over the master plan. The driving force behind this group was the architect Hans Zwimpfer. The group submitted the following proposal: a new underground postal station would be created on the eastern part of the area designated in the master plan. Administrative, service and office buildings would be erected above the postal station. Following a utilisation study by the project group, both the PTT (today Swiss Post) and SBB (Swiss Federal Railways) expressed interest. In 1987, the real estate company Bahnhof Ost AG (I.B.O.) was founded. Its task was to promote and market the project Bahnhof Ost. In 1988, the general contractor agreements were signed. The foundation for the realization of the project Bahnhof Ost had been laid. That same year, planning permission was given for the building site. In 1989 and 1990 the static construction of the new building was determined and the cuboid design was discussed.

By 1991, the Swiss economy was in recession. The postal service questioned the necessity of a new postal station in Basel. The number of railway tracks was reduced from ten to six. The investment was also redistributed between the postal service and I.B.O. The postal service reduced its share from 80 to 70 percent; I.B.O. increased its share from 20 to 30 percent.

Im Frühjahr 1993 präsentiert Hans Zwimpfer der Bauherrschaft das Projekt «Kunst und Architektur». Den zusätzlichen Aufwand der Kunst budgetiert er mit 2,9 Millionen Franken. Bei insgesamt rund 500 Millionen Franken veranschlagten Anlagekosten für das ganze Projekt ist das weniger als 1 Prozent. Im Sommer 1993 verbringt Donald Judd mehrere Tage in Basel.

Am 1. Januar 1994 um 0.30 Uhr wird zu bauen begonnen. Ebenfalls 1994 wird der politisch etwas ins Abseits geratene Masterplan in Euro-Ville Basel umbenannt. Ein Jahr später, 1995, gibt die Post bekannt, dass sie die Posttransporte vermehrt von der Schiene auf die Strasse verlegen wird. Der Planungs- und Bauprozess am Bahnhof Ost läuft weiter. Die Verträge für den Grossaushub, die Pfahlfundation, die Rohbauarbeiten und den Montagebau in Stahl und vorfabrizierte Elemente werden vergeben. Das Jahr 1996 beginnt mit dem Abbruch der Lokdepotanlagen. Im selben Jahr redimensioniert die Post den Postbahnhof, einst das Kernstück des geplanten Bauprojekts, auf drei Gleise. Das Verteilzentrum in Basel soll als Zustellbasis nur noch die umliegende Region beliefern. Die Basler Kreispostdirektion wird aufgehoben.

Das Projekt wird nun ein weiteres Mal überarbeitet. Die Post benötigt nur noch ein Untergeschoss, die übrigen Produktions- und Gewerbeflächen müssen privatwirtschaftlich vermietet werden. Gleichzeitig lässt die Nachfrage nach Büro- und Dienstleistungsräumen, bedingt durch die anhaltende Rezession, weiter nach. Vom ursprünglichen Masterplan, jetzt EuroVille, bleibt folgendes übrig: Die neue Tramführung wird realisiert, die Münchensteinerbrücke ausgebaut, der Centralbahnplatz neu gestaltet sowie eine Fussgängerpasserelle zwischen Gundeldingerquartier und Stadtzentrum ausgeschrieben.

1997 werden die Häuser 82 und 84 an das Informatikunternehmen Systor AG vermietet. Im selben Jahr kauft die Pensionskasse der Kantone Basel-Stadt und Baselland die Häuser 82 und 84. Im Juni 1998 be-

In the spring of 1993, Hans Zwimpfer presented the project "Art and Architecture" to his clients. Additional expenditure for the art was budgeted at 2.9 million Swiss Francs, less than 1 percent of the total calculated budget of about 500 million Francs. In the summer of 1993, Donald Judd spent several days in Basel.

Construction began on January 1, 1994 at 12.30 a.m. Later that year, the master plan, which had been politically sidelined, was renamed Euro-Ville Basel. One year later, in 1995, the postal service announced that it would increasingly shift transport of mail from rail to road. The planning and building process at the East Station continued. The contracts for the excavation, the pile foundation, work on the shell and the steel skeleton and prefabricated elements were assigned. 1996 began with the demolition of the locomotive depots. That same year, the postal service resized the postal station, once the core of the planned building project, to just three tracks. The distribution center in Basel would supply only the surrounding region. The plan for the Basel district postal management office was cancelled.

The project was again revised. The postal service required only a single basement floor at that point; the other production and commercial areas had to be rented to private businesses. At the same time, the demand for office and services space continued to decrease due to the ongoing recession. Of the original master plan, now EuroVille, the following was left: the new tram route would be constructed, the Münchensteiner bridge would be expanded, the central station square would be redesigned, and proposals were tendered for a small pedestrian bridge between the Gundeldinger district and the city center.

In 1997, buildings 82 and 84 were rented to the computer science company Systor AG. In the same year, the pension fund of the cantons Basel-Stadt and Baselland purchased buildings 82 and 84. In June 1998, the College Council of the Fachhochschule beider Basel (Technical

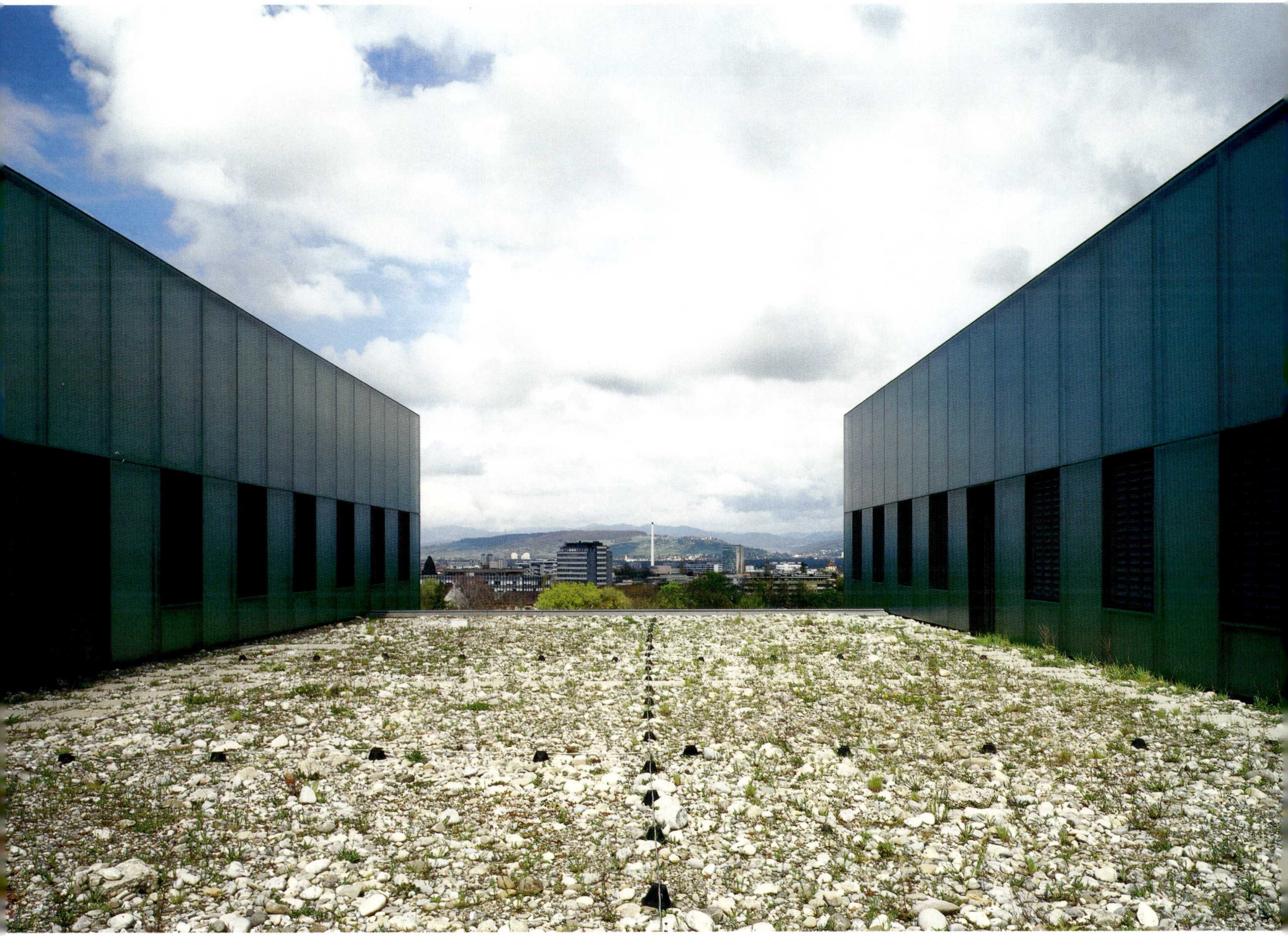

schliesst der Fachhochschulrat beider Basel, die Wirtschaftsabteilung der FHBB im Haus 86 einzumieten. Im April 1999 wird der Postbahnhof in Betrieb genommen. Im Mai des gleichen Jahres wird Haus 90 an das Speditionsunternehmen Danzas vermietet, und ebenfalls 1999 kauft der Trinkaus Europa Immobilienfonds die Häuser 88 und 90, Ascoop Haus 86. Das Haus bekommt nun seinen definitiven Namen: Aus dem Projekt Bahnhof Ost ist über das BusinessCenter Bahnhof Ost das Peter Merian Haus geworden. Im November 1999 beschliessen SBB und I.B.O., das im Osten ans Peter Merian Haus angrenzende Grundstück zu bebauen. Hier entsteht bis ins Jahr 2006 das Jacob Burckhardt Haus. Baubeginn: 1.1.2002.

Am 21. September 2000 wird das Peter Merian Haus offiziell eingeweiht.

University) decided to lease space in number 86 for the financial department of FHBB. In April 1999 the postal station began operating. In May of the same year, building number 90 was rented to the shipping company Danzas, the Trinkaus Europe real estate fund purchased 88 and 90 and Ascoop bought 86. At that point the building was given its name: the project Bahnhof Ost became, via BusinessCenter Bahnhof Ost, Peter Merian House. In November 1999 the SBB and I.B.O. decided to develop the property adjoining Peter Merian House to the east. Construction of Jacob Burckhardt House will begin on January 1, 2002 and continue until its completion in 2006.

Peter Merian House was officially opened on September 21, 2000.

79

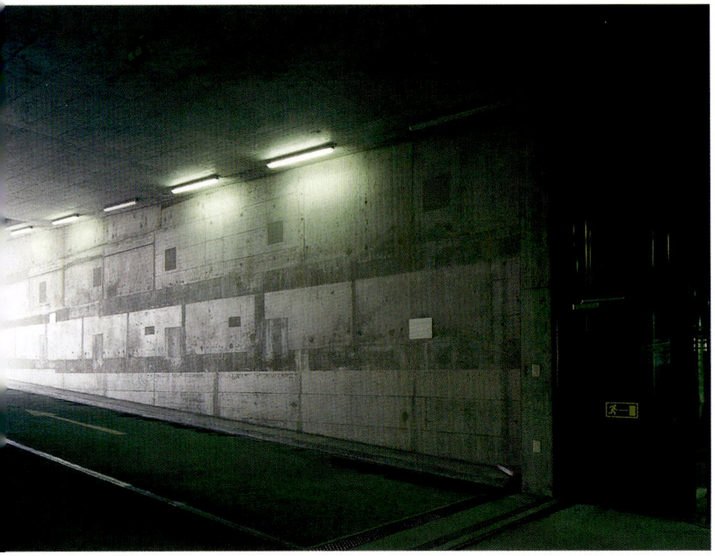

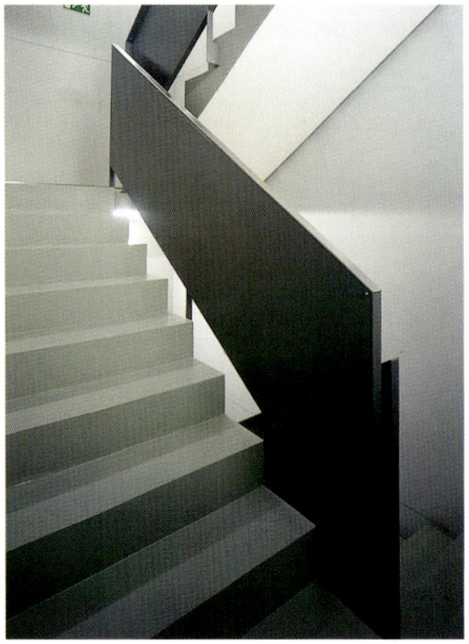

81

ANHANG

BAUTECHNIK, STATIK, FASSADE

Das bauliche Konzept wurde durch folgende Vorgaben und Vorstellungen bestimmt:
– Die grossräumigen Untergeschosse für den Postbetrieb werden von sechs aufgesattelten Häusern überlagert. Die Häuser sind selbständige Eigentumseinheiten mit einem Kernbereich und einer äusseren Fussgängererschliessung. Diese Gliederung erfolgte zu Beginn der neunziger Jahre im Hinblick auf eine etappenweise Realisierung des Bauvorhabens und entsprechend der Nachfrage aus der gesamtökonomischen Situation.
– Die Gebäudestruktur ist offen, gefasst in eine Stahlbetonkonstruktion mit gleich bleibenden Deckenfeldern von 7,30 x 5,92 Meter, runden Vollstahlstützen und einem Ausbauraster von 1,46 x 1,46 Meter.
– Die Nettogeschosshöhe beträgt drei Meter, im Erdgeschoss 3,40 Meter. Das lässt Raum für vielfältige Nutzungen, vom Einzelbüro über Schulzimmer bis zum Vortragssaal.
– Der Grundausbau ist pragmatisch, ein Edelrohbau mit Sichtbetonwänden und -decken.
– Die Glasverkleidung erweist sich im Bahnhofsbereich als flugrostresistent.
– Vor den äusseren Lichthöfen werden Lärmschutzverglasungen angebracht, was für den Grossteil der Dienstleistungsflächen eine natürliche Raumlüftung ermöglicht.

An die Baustatik wurden besondere Anforderungen gestellt:
– Basel ist als erhöht erdbebengefährdet eingestuft. Gebäude mit öffentlicher Nutzung müssen mit grösseren Sicherheitsmargen konstruiert werden. Da im Peter Merian Haus keine tragenden Wände und Kernbereiche bis zu den Fundamenten geführt werden können (wegen des grossräumigen Postbahnhofs in den Untergeschossen), werden die Querkräfte mit der Bildung entsprechender Stützenköpfe gewährleistet.

APPENDIX

CONSTRUCTIONAL ENGINEERING, STATICS, FAÇADE

The construction plan was determined by the following stipulations and ideas:
– The large-scale basement floors for the postal service should be covered by six buildings. The buildings would be independently owned units with their own cores and external pedestrian access. This organization was agreed in the early 1990s with the intention of a multi-phase realization of the building project and in accordance with the demands of the overall economic conditions at that time.
– The building structure should be open with a steel-reinforced concrete frame with even ceiling fields of 7.30 x 5.92 meters; round, solid steel supports, and a development grid of 1.46 x 1.46 meters.
– The net floor height should be 3 meters, or 3.40 meters on the ground floor. This would leave room for various uses, from individual offices to classrooms and lecture halls.
– The basic interiors are pragmatic, a noble shell with fair-faced concrete walls and ceilings.
– The glass cladding should be resistant to airborne rust from around the station.
– Noise protection glazing is mounted before the atria, giving natural ventilation for most of the service areas.

Special stipulations were made for the building statics:
– Basel is rated as a zone with an increased earthquake risk. Buildings for public use must be constructed with greater safety margins. Since none of the supporting walls or core areas in Peter Merian House can be continued down to the foundations (due to the postal station on the basement levels), the lateral forces are secured through the formation of the appropriate column caps.
– Above the 1st basement level the column grid of the office floors is supported by large absorption beams and transferred to the two outer walls and two rows of columns.

– Der Stützenraster der Bürogeschosse wird über dem 1. Untergeschoss mit grossen Abfangträgern übernommen und auf die beiden Aussenwände und zwei Stützenreihen übertragen.
– Um keine Erschütterungsübertragungen vom Postbahnhof zu riskieren, werden die Hauptlasten auf den Stützenreihen mit Pfählen auf Fels fundiert. Dadurch wird der Bahnkörper vom Bau faktisch abgetrennt. Die Vorgabe lautete, dass sich in einem der aufgesattelten Häuser theoretisch ein Vier-Sterne-Hotel befinden können müsste, in dem man vom Nachtbetrieb der Post nichts bemerken würde. Die Vorgabe wurde erfüllt.

Die Fassade und ihre möglichen Materialisierungen wurden eingehend untersucht. Tragende murale Varianten schieden aus, weil die Lasten – wie oben beschrieben – nicht direkt zu den Fundamenten geführt werden konnten. Beobachtungen und Analysen ergaben, dass Bauten im Bahnhofsbereich stark mit Flugrost belastet sind. Glas ist ein diesbezüglich resistentes Material. Die budgetierten Baukosten schlossen aber eine konsequente Curtain-Wall-Fassade aus, denn die Klimatisierung der Bauten, die damit notwendig geworden wäre, hätte nicht nur den Kostenrahmen gesprengt, sondern wäre auch vom Gesetz untersagt worden. Die einfachste Lösung war der klassische Aufbau mit einer vorfabrizierten Betonschale als Kälte- und Wärmespeicher, einer zweischichtigen Aussenisolation, einem Hohlraum und einer Regenschicht – nicht aus Naturstein, Kunststein oder Metall, sondern aus Glas. Dennoch entstand kein Glashaus, sondern ein mit Glas verkleidetes Haus. Zusammen mit Donald Judd einigten sich die Architekten auf die Farbe Grün mit einem gewissen Blauanteil, damit der Farbton, auch wenn die Fassade einmal verschmutzt wäre, nicht ins Olivgrüne kippen würde. Blieb die Frage der Glasstrukturierung: auf keinen Fall sollte der Baukörper die Umgebung, indem er sie in der Glasfassade spiegelte, mit seiner Wucht beherrschen. Flussglas erfüllte diese Anforderung, war aber als Handelsware nicht greifbar, so dass in einem langwierigen Prozess entsprechende Glasmuster angefertigt werden mussten.

– In order to avoid the possibility of shock transfer from the postal station, the main loads of the rows of columns are anchored to the bedrock with piles. The station volume is thereby physically separated from the building. The stipulation was that a four-star hotel could theoretically be built on top of the postal station, and the noise of the nightly underground activities would need to be damped. This stipulation was fulfilled.

The façade and possible ways of realizing it were examined thoroughly. Variations that integrated the façade into a supporting wall were ruled out since the loads – as described above – could not be transferred directly to the foundations. Observations and analyses showed that buildings in the area of the station are highly susceptible to the build up of films of rust. Glass is a resistant material in this respect. The budgeted cost of building, however, excluded a continuous curtain façade wall because it would have required air conditioning, which would not only have pushed the project over budget but would also have been against the law. The simplest solution would have been a classic construction with a prefabricated concrete shell for passive cold and heat storage, a two-layered exterior insulation, a hollow space and a rain layer – in glass rather than natural or artificial stone or metal. And yet it was not a glass building that was created, but a building encased in glass. Together with Donald Judd, the architects agreed on the color, green with a slightly blueish hue, to prevent it from turning olive green should the façade later become dirty. There remained the issue of how to structure the glass, because the mass of the building volume should not dominate the surrounding environment by reflecting it. Alluvial glass fulfilled this condition but was not available as a commercial product. The appropriate glass patterns were painstakingly produced specially for this project.

The low-tech principle, providing a noble shell with hollow floors for distributing media services to the occupants, without fixed ceiling light in-

Das Low-tech-Prinzip, das dem Mieter einen Edelrohbau mit durchgehenden Hohlböden für die Medienverteilung anbietet, ohne fest installierte Deckenbeleuchtung und insgesamt mit einer offenen Baustruktur für eine vielfältige und variable Nutzung, wurde zu Beginn der neunziger Jahre entwickelt. Bei der Vermietung der Bauten hat es sich bewährt und wird heute von den Nutzern geschätzt.

Die Planung eines so grossen Gebäudes mit langen Vorlaufzeiten für Einzonung, Projektierung und gegebenenfalls zu überstehenden wirtschaftlichen Durststrecken ist immer eine Planung für unbekannte Nutzer. Es liegt beim Architekten, Trends aufzuspüren, um zum Zeitpunkt des Verkaufs oder der Vermietung Nutzerwünsche erfüllen zu können. Dabei ist es schliesslich eine grundsätzliche Frage, ob der Architekt an die offene Entwicklung der Ansprüche glaubt, also auch an deren Wandelbarkeit, oder ob er sich selbst als Zeitdokument betonieren will.

Als schwierige Schnittstelle hat sich der Innenausbau der Lichthöfe erwiesen. Der vom Architekten vorgegebene Bau, der integral in die «Gestaltungshoheit» der Künstlerinnen und Künstler übergeben worden war, kollidierte teilweise mit den zusätzlichen Dekorationswünschen der Mieter. Konsequenterweise wird beim Jacob Burckhardt Haus das Thema Kunst und Architektur ins Äussere verlegt.

stallations and with an open building structure for versatile and variable use, was developed at the beginning of the 1990s. It has proved to be invaluable in renting the buildings, and is still appreciated by the users.

Planning such a large building with long lag times for obtaining planning permission, project complications and possible economic difficulties inevitably means planning for unknown users. It is up to the architect to sense trends in order to meet the needs of the users at the time of sale or lease. In the end, the fundamental issue is whether the architect believes in the open development of standards, including their mutability, or whether he wants to be set in concrete as a record of the times.

The interior design of the atria turned out to be a difficult interface. The building as stipulated by the architect, which was given over to the "design sovereignty" of the artists, sometimes clashed with the additional decorative wishes of the tenants. As a consequence, the theme of art and architecture will be moved to the exterior in the building of the Jacob Burckhardt House.

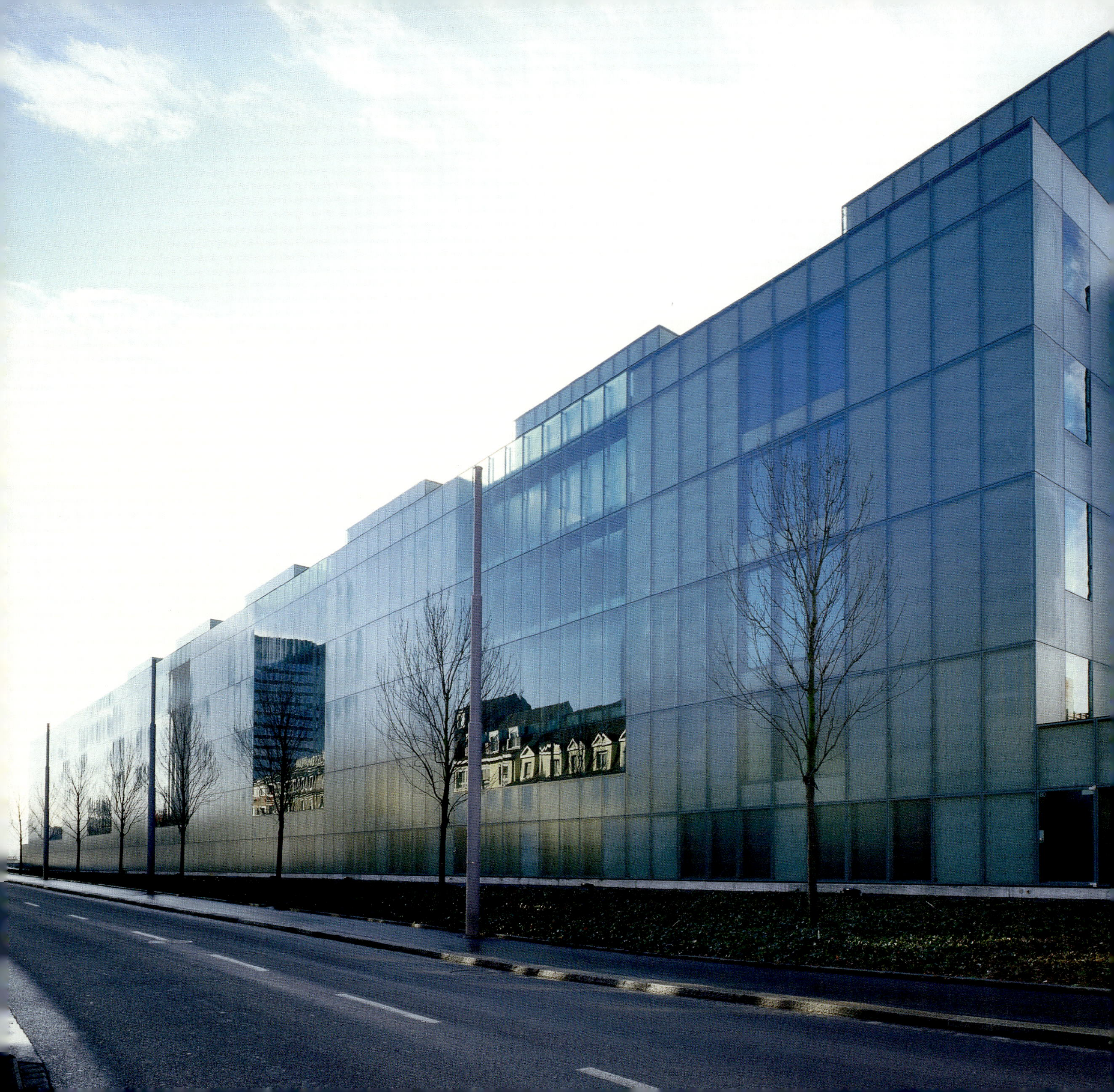

TECHNISCHE DATEN

Bruttogeschossfläche insgesamt: 85 000 m²

Kubus insgesamt: 370 000 m³

Stahl insgesamt: 8200 t
Stahl-Armierung: 4600 t
Beton: 40 000 m³
Aushub: 181 000 m³
Schalung: 126 000 m²

Fassade, Fläche insgesamt: 24 000 m²
Fassade, Anzahl Glasplatten: 4900 Stück à ca. 125 kg

Fussweg Roni Horn: 1500 m²

KOSTEN

Peter Merian Haus, inkl. Postbahnhof: 380 Mio CHF
Zufahrtstunnel: 80 Mio CHF
Insgesamt: 460 Mio CHF

TECHNICAL DATA

Gross floor area: 85,000 m² overall

Total cubic space: 370,000 m³

Total steel: 8,200 t
Steel reinforcement rods: 4,600 t
Concrete: 40,000 m³
Excavated earth: 181,000 m³
Formwork: 126,000 m²

Façade, total surface: 24,000 m²
Façade, number of glass panels: 4,900 panels of approx. 125 kg each

Roni Horn walkway: 1,500 m²

COST

Peter Merian Haus, incl. postal station: CHF 380 million
Access tunnel: CHF 80 million
Total: CHF 460 million

Situation | Site plan

Ansicht Süd | View from the South

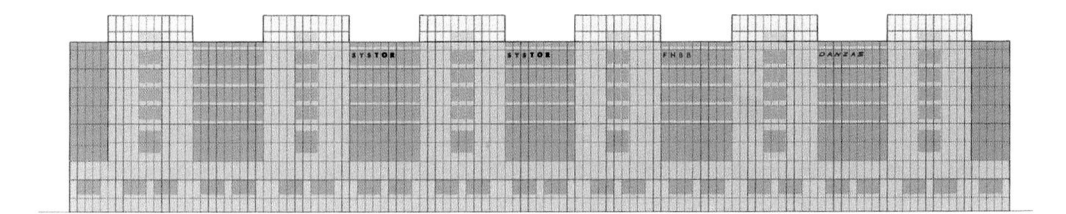

Ansicht Ost | View from the East

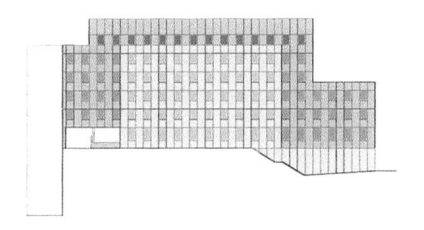

Ansicht Nord | View from the North

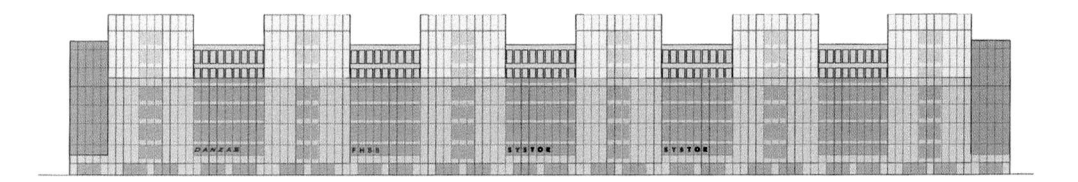

Ansicht West | View from the West

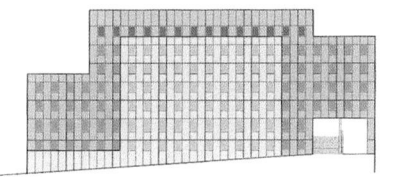

0 2 4 6 8 10   20   30   40   50

Grundriss Niveau 1 Eingangsgeschoss / Fussweg | Ground plan level 1 / walkway

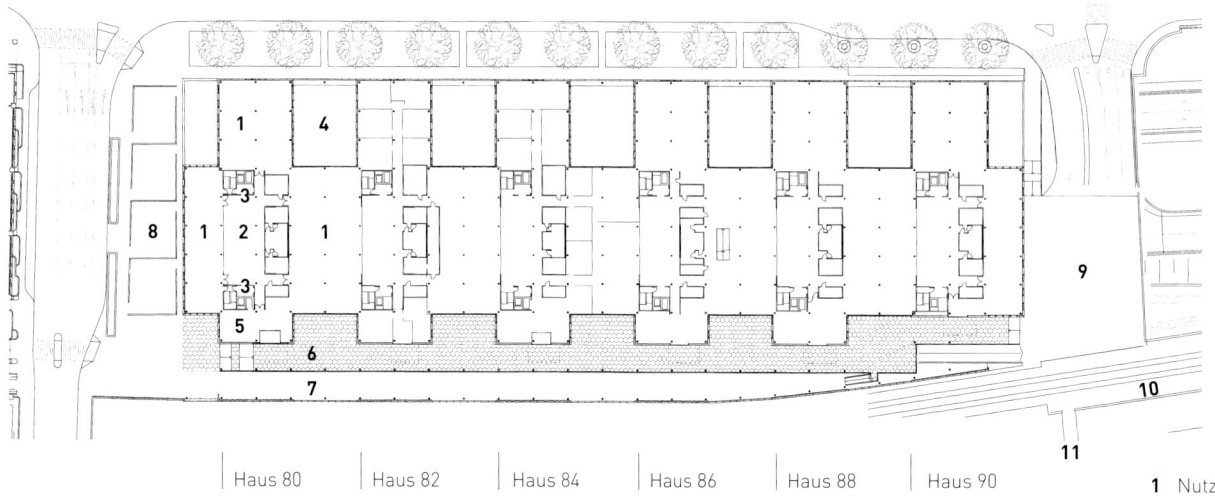

| Haus 80 | Haus 82 | Haus 84 | Haus 86 | Haus 88 | Haus 90 |

Grundriss Niveau 2/3 Normalgeschoss | Ground plan level 2/3 standard floor

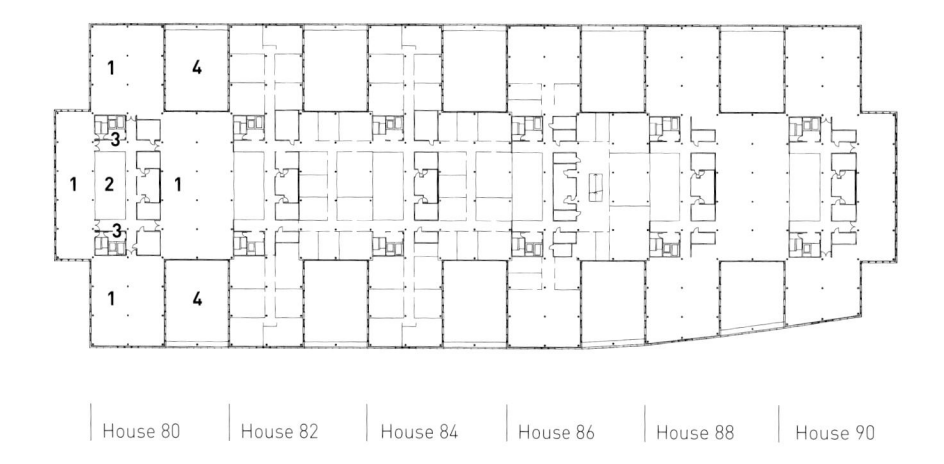

| House 80 | House 82 | House 84 | House 86 | House 88 | House 90 |

1 Nutzfläche | Useable area
2 Lichthof | Atrium
3 Vertikalerschliessung | Vertical development
4 Lärmschutzhof | Noise protection yard
5 Eingang / Windfang | Entrance / fly brake
6 Fussgängerweg | Pedestrian walkway
7 Fahrradweg | Bicycle track
8 Skulpturengarten / temporäre Installationen | Sculpture garden / temporary installations
9 Vorplatz Ost (Gestaltung mit Bau 2. Etappe) | Forecourt East (design with building 2nd stage)
10 Tramhaltestelle 10/11 | Tram stop 10/11
11 Gundelipasserelle | Gundeli passageway

Schnitte | Sections

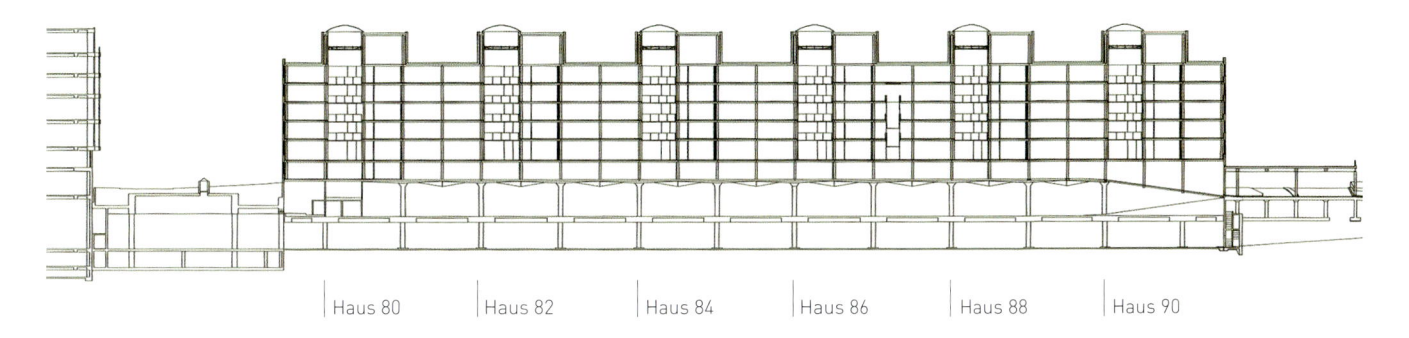

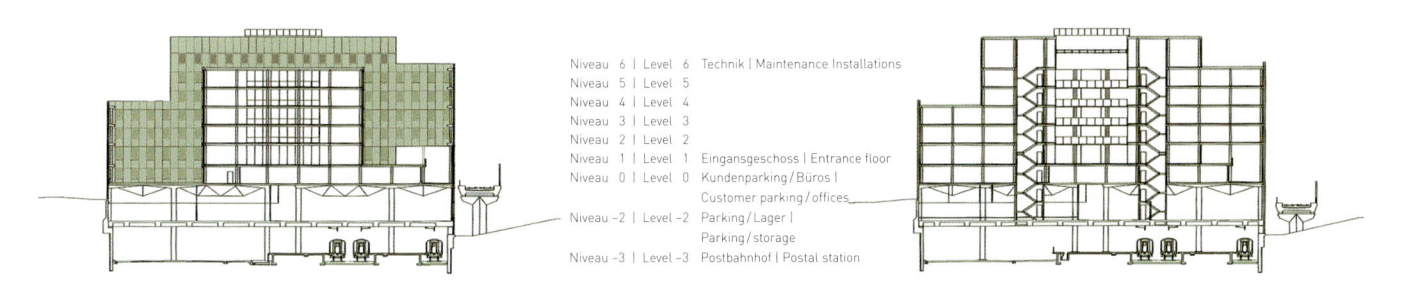

| Haus 80 | Haus 82 | Haus 84 | Haus 86 | Haus 88 | Haus 90 |

Niveau 6 | Level 6 Technik | Maintenance Installations
Niveau 5 | Level 5
Niveau 4 | Level 4
Niveau 3 | Level 3
Niveau 2 | Level 2
Niveau 1 | Level 1 Eingansgeschoss | Entrance floor
Niveau 0 | Level 0 Kundenparking / Büros |
Customer parking / offices
Niveau −2 | Level −2 Parking / Lager |
Parking / storage
Niveau −3 | Level −3 Postbahnhof | Postal station

0 2 4 6 8 10   20   30   40   50

BETEILIGTE KÜNSTLERINNEN UND KÜNSTLER

Donald Judd, Fassadendesign
Roni Horn, «Yous in You», Fussweg mit Sitzbänken

Brigitte Kowanz, «Light is what we see», Lichthof, Haus 80
Ursula Mumenthaler, «Le champ bleu», Lichthof, Haus 82
Pipilotti Rist, «Geist des Stroms», Lichthof, Haus 84
François Morellet, «Bogen, Sehne, Licht» und «Bogen, Sehne, Strich», Lichthof und Treppenbrüstung, Haus 86
Beat Zoderer, «Räumliches Aquarell», Lichthof, Haus 88
Hans Danuser, «Nah und fern», Lichthof, Haus 90

Begleitende Kunstprojekte:
Balthasar Burkhard, Fotomappe Lokdepot, mit dem Essay «Die Mütze» von Martin Roda Becher
Rogelio López Cuenca, Signaltafeln zur Markierung der Baustelle
Irene Grundel, Litfasssäule mit Mosaikauge
Anne Hoffmann, Plakatgrafik
Guido Nussbaum, Litfasssäule mit Bautafeln
Rudolf Tschudin, Litfasssäule mit Tänzer

Eröffnungsperformance:
Ruth-Lucía Baumgartner mit Influx Tanzkompanie, Tanzperformance «Le champ bleu» (18. November 1999)

Kunstprojekte auf dem Vorplatz:
Eric Hattan, «Urbanes Eis», Vorplatz (November 1999 bis Februar 2000)
Martin Blum und Haimo Ganz, «Glaspyramiden», Vorplatz (März 2000 bis Dezember 2000)

PARTICIPATING ARTISTS

Donald Judd, façade design
Roni Horn, "Yous in You", walkway with benches

Brigitte Kowanz, "Light is what we see", atrium, building 80
Ursula Mumenthaler, "Le champ bleu", atrium, building 82
Pipilotti Rist, "Geist des Stroms", atrium, building 84
François Morellet, "Bogen, Sehne, Licht" and "Bogen, Sehne, Strich", atrium and staircase parapet, building 86
Beat Zoderer, "Räumliches Aquarell", atrium, building 88
Hans Danuser, "Nah und fern", atrium, building 90

Accompanying Art Projects:
Balthasar Burkhard, photo portfolio locomotive depot, with the essay "Die Mütze" by Martin Roda Becher
Rogelio López Cuenca, construction signs to mark the building site
Irene Grundel, advertising pillar with mosaic eye
Anne Hoffmann, poster graphics
Guido Nussbaum, advertising pillar with building signs
Rudolf Tschudin, advertising pillar with dancer

Opening Performance:
Ruth-Lucía Baumgartner with Influx Tanzkompanie, Dance performance "Le champ bleu" (18 November 1999)

Art Projects on the Forecourt:
Eric Hattan, "Urbanes Eis", forecourt (November 1999 to February 2000)
Martin Blum and Haimo Ganz, "Glaspyramiden", forecourt (March to December 2000)

1986-2000

Planning:
Gesamtleitung: Hans Zwimpfer

Generalplaner: Projektgruppe Bahnhof Ost; Leitung: Rudolf Zimmer

Architektur und Planung: Zwimpfer Partner Architekten
Bürgin Nissen Wentzlaff Architekten (bis 1995)

Hans Zwimpfer, Edi Bürgin, Timothy O. Nissen, Ernst Zimmer

Lucien Brom, Pascal Essigmann, Christian Geser, Jacqueline Goetschy, Mirco Morassi, Tobias Nissen, Markus Rütimann

Modellbau: Sidney Bannier

Baumanagement: Bruno Buser, Christian Hauser, Hanspeter Lüttin, Konrad Kissling, Hans Dalle Carbonare

Statik- und Verkehrsplanung: Rapp AG, WGG Ingenieure
René Guillod, Dr. Matthias Rapp, Adrian Kunz, Rolf Nachbur, Jürg Renz, Marcel Schmidli

Fachplaner Haustechnik: Bogenschütz AG, Selmoni AG, Waldhauser Haustechnik
Urs W. Feuerlein, Daniel Stolz, Werner Waldhauser, Marc Baumgart, Patrick Kiefer, Marianne Kistler, Gerd Schwittay, Mario Régis

EDV, Kommunikation: CAD Lucien Brom, Andreas Honegger

Finanzmanagement und Administration: Philippe Burri, Christine Bucher, Liselotte Christen, Esther Genner, Rosmarie Krähenbühl, Christine Schifferle

1986–2000

Planning:
Overall project management: Hans Zwimpfer

General planning: Project Group Bahnhof Ost; Direction: Rudolf Zimmer

Architecture and planning: Zwimpfer Partner Architekten
Bürgin Nissen Wentzlaff Architekten (until 1995)

Hans Zwimpfer, Edi Bürgin, Timothy O. Nissen, Ernst Zimmer

Lucien Brom, Pascal Essigmann, Christian Geser, Jacqueline Goetschy, Mirco Morassi, Tobias Nissen, Markus Rütimann

Model making: Sidney Bannier

Building management: Bruno Buser, Christian Hauser, Hanspeter Lüttin, Konrad Kissling, Hans Dalle Carbonare

Statics and traffic planning: Rapp AG, WGG Ingenieure
René Guillod, Dr. Matthias Rapp, Adrian Kunz, Rolf Nachbur, Jürg Renz, Marcel Schmidli

Technical planning building technology: Bogenschütz AG, Selmoni AG, Waldhauser Haustechnik
Urs W. Feuerlein, Daniel Stolz, Werner Waldhauser, Marc Baumgart, Patrick Kiefer, Marianne Kistler, Gerd Schwittay, Mario Régis

IT, communications: CAD Lucien Brom, Andreas Honegger

Financial management and administration: Philippe Burri, Christine Bucher, Liselotte Christen, Esther Genner, Rosmarie Krähenbühl, Christine Schifferle

Bauherrschaft:

- Die Schweizerische Post, Bern: Andreas Brönnimann, Max Hintermann, Hans Läderach, Dr. Bruno Mäder, Nick Roth, Jürg Ryser, Ueli Straub, Urs Walz
- I.B.O. Immobiliengesellschaft Bahnhof Ost AG, Basel: Dr. Christoph Stutz, Dr. Albrecht Girsberger, Dr. Richard Peter, Dr. Michael Pfeifer, Dr. Matthias Rapp, Dr. Rolf Soiron, Dr. Amédéo Wermelinger, Hans Zwimpfer
- Schweizerische Bundesbahnen (SBB), Kreisdirektion II, Luzern: Dr. Amédéo Wermelinger, Dr. Christoph Caviezel, Andreas Fischer, Urs Martin Koch, Joseph Rogger
- Swisscom AG, Bern: René Graf, Herbert Erni, Markus Kuonen, Jürg Thomet

Kunst und Architektur:

Hans Zwimpfer, Franziska Baetcke, Christian Geser, Thomas Kellein, Elisabeth Masé, Hortensia von Roda, Dominik Soiron

Eigentümer:

- Haus 80: SPS Swiss Prime Site AG, Olten
- Haus 82: Pensionskasse des Basler Staatspersonals / Pensionskasse Basel-Land
- Haus 84: Pensionskasse des Basler Staatspersonals / Pensionskasse Basel-Land
- Haus 86: Pensionskasse der Ascoop, Bern
- Haus 88: HSBC Trinkaus & Burkhardt Immobilien GmbH, Düsseldorf
- Haus 90: HSBC Trinkaus & Burkhardt Immobilien GmbH, Düsseldorf

Clients:

- Swiss Post, Bern: Andreas Brönnimann, Max Hintermann, Hans Läderach, Dr. Bruno Mäder, Nick Roth, Jürg Ryser, Ueli Straub, Urs Walz
- I.B.O. Immobiliengesellschaft Bahnhof Ost AG, Basel: Dr. Christoph Stutz, Dr. Albrecht Girsberger, Dr. Richard Peter, Dr. Michael Pfeifer, Dr. Matthias Rapp, Dr. Rolf Soiron, Dr. Amédéo Wermelinger, Hans Zwimpfer
- Swiss Federal Railways (SBB), Kreisdirektion II, Lucerne: Dr. Amédéo Wermelinger, Dr. Christoph Caviezel, Andreas Fischer, Urs Martin Koch, Joseph Rogger
- Swisscom AG, Bern: René Graf, Herbert Erni, Markus Kuonen, Jürg Thomet

Art and architecture:

Hans Zwimpfer, Franziska Baetcke, Christian Geser, Thomas Kellein, Elisabeth Masé, Hortensia von Roda, Dominik Soiron

Owners:

- Building 80: SPS Swiss Prime Site AG, Olten
- Building 82: Pensionskasse des Basler Staatspersonals / Pensionskasse Basel-Land
- Building 84: Pensionskasse des Basler Staatspersonals / Pensionskasse Basel-Land
- Building 86: Pensionskasse der Ascoop, Bern
- Building 88: HSBC Trinkaus & Burkhardt Immobilien GmbH, Düsseldorf
- Building 90: HSBC Trinkaus & Burkhardt Immobilien GmbH, Düsseldorf

Mieter:
- Haus 80: Obtree Technologies Inc.
- Haus 82: Systor AG
- Haus 84: Systor AG
- Haus 86: Fachhochschule beider Basel (FHBB), Wirtschaftsinformatik-Schule Schweiz (WISS)
- Haus 88: Danzas AG
- Haus 90: Danzas AG, Alcatel AG, SBB Cargo

Die Protokollhefte zum Projekt «Kunst und Architektur» im Bahnhof Ost, Basel, dokumentieren die Zusammenarbeit zwischen Künstlern und Architekten am Peter Merian Haus. In Form von Gesprächen, Briefwechseln, Fotos, Plänen, Skizzen und Modellen geben sie Einblick in ein ungewöhnliches Kunstengagement. Die Protokollhefte 1–6 sind im Verlag Lars Müller in Baden erschienen.

- Protokollheft 1: Ein Projekt ist keine Insel. Die Geschichte des Projekts Bahnhof Ost
- Protokollheft 2: Die Fassade soll ein Zeichen setzen. Dokumentation der Zusammenarbeit zwischen den Architekten und Donald Judd
- Protokollheft 3: Mehr als nur Kunst am Bau. Das Konzept «Kunst und Architektur» und erste Arbeiten
- Protokollheft 4: Ein Stück Island in Basel. Roni Horns Gestaltung der Passage für Fussgänger und Velofahrer
- Protokollheft 5: Kowanz Mumenthaler Rist. Die Gestaltung der sechs inneren Lichthöfe (Teil 1)
- Protokollheft 6: Morellet Zoderer Danuser. Die Gestaltung der sechs inneren Lichthöfe (Teil 2). Ruth-Lucía Baumgartner mit Influx Tanzkompanie, «Le champ bleu». Eric Hattan, «Urbanes Eis»

Tenants:
- Building 80: Obtree Technologies Inc.
- Building 82: Systor AG
- Building 84: Systor AG
- Building 86: Fachhochschule beider Basel (FHBB), Wirtschaftsinformatik-Schule Schweiz (WISS)
- Building 88: Danzas AG
- Building 90: Danzas AG, Alcatel AG, SBB Cargo

The protocol books of the project "Art and Architecture" in the East Station, Basel, document the collaboration between artists and architects at Peter Merian House. Through conversations, letters, photographs, plans, sketches and models, they offer an insight into an unusual commitment to art. Protocol books 1–6 were published by Verlag Lars Müller in Baden.

- Protokollheft 1: Ein Projekt ist keine Insel. Die Geschichte des Projekts Bahnhof Ost
- Protokollheft 2: Die Fassade soll ein Zeichen setzen. Dokumentation der Zusammenarbeit zwischen den Architekten und Donald Judd
- Protokollheft 3: Mehr als nur Kunst am Bau. Das Konzept "Kunst und Architektur" und erste Arbeiten
- Protokollheft 4: Ein Stück Island in Basel. Roni Horns Gestaltung der Passage für Fussgänger und Velofahrer
- Protokollheft 5: Kowanz Mumenthaler Rist. Die Gestaltung der sechs inneren Lichthöfe (Teil 1)
- Protokollheft 6: Morellet Zoderer Danuser. Die Gestaltung der sechs inneren Lichthöfe (Teil 2). Ruth-Lucía Baumgartner with Influx Tanzkompanie, "Le champ bleu". Eric Hattan, "Urbanes Eis"